# CAIRO PAPERS IN SOCIAL SCIENCE
VOLUME 35                                NUMBER 2

# International Migration in the Euro-Mediterranean Region

Edited by
Ibrahim Awad

Contributors
Maysa Ayoub        Angelos Dalachanis
Gerda Heck         Alexandra Parrs
Gerasimos Tsourapas    Joseph John Viscomi

THE AMERICAN UNIVERSITY IN CAIRO PRESS
CAIRO   NEW YORK

Cover photo: courtesy of Amani AbdelBari

This paperback edition first published in 2023 by
The American University in Cairo Press
113 Sharia Kasr el Aini, Cairo, Egypt
420 Lexington Avenue, Suite 1644, New York, NY 10170
www.aucpress.com

First published in an electronic edition in 2019

Copyright © 2019, 2023 by the American University in Cairo Press

All rights reserved. No part of this publication may be reproduced, stored in a retrieval system, or transmitted in any form or by any means, electronic, mechanical, photocopying, recording, or otherwise, without the prior written permission of the publisher.

ISBN 978 1 649 03227 0

Library of Congress Cataloging-in-Publication Data applied for

1 2 3 4 5   27 26 25 24

Designed by Adam el-Sehemy

# Contents

1 Introduction: Migration and Refugee 'Crisis' in the Euro-Mediterranean Region: Which 'Crisis'? And for Whom?  1
   *Ibrahim Awad*

2 Between Italy and Egypt: Migrating Histories and Political Genealogies  15
   *Joseph John Viscomi*

3 Kaleidoscopic Out-Migration: The Departure of Foreigners from Mid Twentieth Century Egypt  34
   *Angelos Dalachanis*

4 Waiting in Izmir: Syrians in the Aegean Region after the "EU–Turkey Deal"  55
   *Gerda Heck*

5 Culturalized, Gendered, and Fractured Approaches to the Integration of Refugees in Brussels  71
   *Alexandra Parrs*

6 Diaspora Politics in Illiberal Contexts: Authoritarianism and Cross-Border Mobility in the Modern Middle East  90
   *Gerasimos Tsourapas*

7   Interest Groups and Refugee Policy-Making:
    The Case of Germany                                      117
    *Maysa Ayoub*

About the Contributors                                       142

CHAPTER 1

# Introduction
# Migration and Refugee 'Crisis' in the Euro-Mediterranean Region: Which 'Crisis'? And for Whom?

*Ibrahim Awad*

In spring 2016, *Cairo Papers in Social Science* decided to dedicate their 25th annual symposium the following year to the subject of "International Migration in the Mediterranean Basin." The Center for Migration and Refugee Studies (CMRS) found that this could not have been more timely, in line with the habitual response of *Cairo Papers* to the most pressing social issues in public debate. Spring 2016 witnessed the height of discussions and alarm on the European side of the Mediterranean over the flows of displaced people reaching Europe by land and sea. "The migration and refugee 'crisis'" in the Euro-Mediterranean region was coined as an expression. Before describing the chapters in this issue of *Cairo Papers*, this introduction will present some reflections about the 'crisis' and then about the normal situation to which the region reverted. The reasons for writing 'crisis' in quotation marks will become apparent in the discussion below.

## 'Crisis'

I first take up the term 'crisis.' This is used so often that its meaning has been unquestioned. People who use the term and people who are the objects of the 'crisis' discourse have stopped asking themselves about its meaning. A major, highly respected, international not-for-profit, non-governmental organization concerned with 'crises' was created in the mid 1990s and has acquired increasing importance in the last decade: the International Crisis Group (ICG). The followers of the worthy efforts of the ICG are bewildered by its confusion of 'crises' with 'conflicts,' as when it identifies the crises to be watched in 2016 or 2017. In the last ten years alone, the term 'crisis' has been particularly used in two situations: the "'global economic 'crisis'" and the "migration and refugee 'crisis.'" Therefore, the question arises: what is a 'crisis'?

Linguistically speaking, many definitions of the term exist. Only a few are spelled out here. It is a time of intense difficulty or danger, or a time when a difficult or important decision is made. It is also a turning point in a sequence of events at which the trend of all future events, for better or for worse, is determined. In international affairs of social, economic, or political character, one definition of 'crisis' is that it is a condition of instability or danger leading to a decisive change. Three years after the peak of the alarm in 2015–2016, the flows of 'crisis' claims have sensibly receded. I will return later to the definition of 'crisis,' especially that of 'crisis' in international affairs, to see whether it actually applies to the migration and refugee movements of recent years in the Mediterranean basin.

## Mediterranean Region

For geographers, the region centered upon a sea includes its hinterland. Therefore, the Mediterranean region includes the basin of the Mediterranean Sea and its hinterland. This is the definition adopted by the European Union (EU), in any case. The EU view of the Mediterranean thus encompasses Jordan, which is not a coastal state. When the 5+5 countries of the Western Mediterranean Basin meet, they include Portugal to the north and Mauritania to the south, both non-coastal countries. The Mediterranean also includes Europe as a whole, since European integration does not allow Mediterranean Europe to act on its own. The attitude of Germany and others toward the original idea of the Union for the Mediterranean (UfM) and integrated policies such as trade policy are the best witnesses to that.

Having summarily defined 'crisis' and delineated the space where it is assumed to have unfolded, I will review the migration and refugee movements in this space since 2011. The numbers involved are known and easily accessible. The review focuses on trends and directions rather than on detailed statistics. Two sub-periods are identified: 2011–2013 and 2014–2016.

## Migration and Refugee Movements 2011–2013

The Awakening of several Arab countries on the southern and eastern rims of the Mediterranean in the winter of 2010–2011 raised concerns, particularly in European countries, about the migration flows it could engender. It was believed that political instability and the economic slowdown that would ensue would be at the origin of large migration flows. A senior political figure in the EU warned of migration flows of "Biblical dimensions." The fact is that, despite some initial irregular movements of limited size in spring 2011, the large flows did not materialize (Awad 2013). Rather than toward the north, the Arab Awakening generated population movements at the east of the Mediterranean basin, within the Arab Middle East region and in its immediate neighborhood. In Syria, revolt against the political regime in power soon turned into open civil strife. Refugee movements to bordering Jordan and Lebanon started and then accelerated. They also reached neighboring Turkey and Egypt. Considering the volumes of the moving populations and those of the bordering countries, specifically Jordan and Lebanon, the Syrian refugee movements stood out as unprecedented.

As revolt against authoritarianism and arbitrariness reached Libya and toppled the Gaddafi regime, other types of population movements took shape in 2011–2012. These were movements of Egyptians, Tunisians, and nationals of African countries south of Libya fleeing the violence and returning home. Followers of Gaddafi also sought refuge to the east and west, in Egypt and Tunisia. A third type was that of hundreds of thousands of migrant workers, mainly of Asian origin, who also fled to Egypt and Tunisia and, from there, were flown to their countries of origin.

It is apparent from this brief review that in 2011–2013 movements out of Syria were to Jordan and Lebanon and, in a secondary order of magnitude, to Egypt and Turkey. Movements out of Libya were to Egypt and Tunisia. According to UNHCR numbers, in Lebanon one out of five nationals and residents was a Syrian refugee. In Jordan, some 10 per cent were Syrian refugees. These flows were added to previous refugees, such as from Palestine and Iraq, hosted in the two countries. If 'crisis' there was, it certainly affected the Middle East, specifically the Arab Middle East.

## Migration and Refugee Movements in 2014–2016

Having been increasingly militarized, the Syrian civil strife continued producing refugees. Jordan and Lebanon became saturated, and securing livelihoods more and more difficult. In Egypt, the political changes of 2013 preempted the arrival of more Syrian refugees and prompted some among those already in the country to leave. Iraqis who had taken refuge in Syria returned to their home country, and with them Syrians, especially ethnic Kurds, also moved in the direction of Iraq. Most new waves, however, flowed to Turkey. In 2011–2012, Turkey had felt capable of managing the tens of thousands of refugees who had entered its regions bordering on Syria. It did not need international assistance to put in place decent living conditions for the Syrian refugees. But as of 2014, the volume of Syrian refugees to Turkey rapidly increased. They soon exceeded 1 million, 1.5 million, 2 million, 2.5 million, and finally reached 2.7 million in 2015. At that point, Turkey required international assistance. With only its own resources it could not ensure these millions the same decent living conditions it had put in place for the tens of thousands in 2011–2012.

Lebanon, Jordan, Iraq, Egypt, and now Turkey having become too narrow, refugees from Syria overflowed to neighboring Europe, seeking protection and livelihoods there. Incidentally, this showed how judicious the EU had been when, starting in 2003, it considered the Mediterranean region as falling in its neighborhood and dedicated to it the largest part of the European Neighborhood Policy (ENP). Numbers of refugees rapidly increased. The figure of one million who reached Europe in 2015 was emphasized time and again. However, it has to be measured against the 508 million population of the EU or the 82 million of Germany alone. In Europe, refugees from Syria would amount to 1/508 of the population, as opposed to one-fourth relative to the Lebanese population.

Prevented by various maneuvers from legally accessing territories of the EU member states where, according to international refugee law, they have the right to seek protection, refugees resorted to smugglers at land and sea and risked their lives in their attempt to salvage them. The EU member states were divided first about keeping their borders open, and later in respect of jointly shouldering responsibility for the refugees. Some member states categorically rejected any mandatory repartition of refugees or participation in financially supporting them. The Syrian refugee flows soon revealed strains, a 'crisis,' in the very same European integration process. No one could have ever thought of population movements from the neighborhood as a possible threat to the 'precious' ideal of European integration. The populations of individual member states were also divided, some welcoming refugees and supporters of international cooperation and solidarity, and others totally hostile and xenophobic. Political cultures were disparate not only between member states but also within each of them. Nationalism and populism were reinvigorated as never before since the end of the Second World War. Strains and divisions between and within the EU member states were harbingers of changes, possibly decisive for European integration. Decisive change as a result of instability or danger is a criterion of a crisis in international political, social, and economic affairs, as stated above. The growing rift between member states in central and western Europe is one unmistakable sign of such change. The formation of the Euroskeptical, far-right, populist and anti-immigrant coalition government in Italy in June 2018 is another such sign.

Despite the negative public discourse, Syrians were far from alone in heading to northern and western Europe through the Aegean Sea and the west Balkan routes. Eritreans, nationals of central and west African countries, and even of Asian countries, as well as citizens of European countries in the west Balkans, such as Albania, Bosnia, and Serbia, mixed with the flows of Syrian refugees. Their causes for moving were obviously of mixed nature, both political and economic.

Seizing the opportunity of the power vacuum and state collapse in Libya, the Central Mediterranean route to Italy became much more important. Movements from Libya were mostly made up of migrants who originated in African and even Asian countries. Much smaller flows departed from Egypt. Some refugees, such as from Eritrea, were among the flows, but the vast majority were migrants. The causes for these movements were mainly economic. To control the movements, patrolling of the sea was reinforced, and smuggling, considered as responsible for the flows, was combatted using military means for the first time.

After this brief review of migration and refugee movements in the Mediterranean region, questions arise. Is there or are there crises? In what respect, and for whom?

There are crises and other underlying, long-standing or deeper conflicts, which are sometimes not distinguished in public discourse. The confusion of the ICG discourse about crises is understandable. The term 'crisis' seems to justify the use of exceptional measures to counter its object: the migration and refugee movements. These exceptional measures included the militarization of anti-smuggling efforts in the Mediterranean, building a fence to keep asylum seekers from accessing the territory of a specific country, and even calls for modifying the international protection regime and watering down its provisions.

If there is a 'crisis,' it is no doubt in Lebanon and Jordan, given their migration rates, that is, the proportion of refugees in their populations. In contrast, in Europe, one refugee or migrant in 508 people cannot be considered a 'crisis' by any stretch of imagination. This is not to deny the anxiety and the sense of economic and social insecurity felt by large segments of nationals of EU member states. It is only a call for searching for the authentic origins of this anxiety and insecurity. Stopping flows and even removal of all migrants will certainly not remedy them. It is also an appeal for the coordination of migration, development, humanitarian, and employment policies, which should be subjects of consultation and joint formulation, where appropriate, between countries of destination in the north and countries of origin on the southern coast of the Mediterranean and beyond.

An implicit question remains unstated. There may be human tragedies in the Middle East and misery in Africa and Asia, but what responsibility does Europe have for them? The answer is that Europe and the international system as a whole must certainly share in the responsibility for these tragedies and misery. The Middle East specifically is a sub-system of the international system. Any ills of the sub-system are also those of the system. It is astonishing that this needs to be asserted. The movements from the Middle East to the European neighborhood should have been sufficient to bring this point home. The failure to address tragedies in the Middle East translates into undesirable consequences for European countries. These consequences are not only the arrival of refugees and migrants. They are also the increasing manifestations of the 'crisis' of European integration. The way to address the tragedies is through international cooperation, precisely in the form of opportunities for livelihood and protection. Far from undermining the

# Migration and Refugee Movements in 2014–2016

countries receiving them, protection of refugees preserves the international system and, as a consequence, the nation-states that constitute it.

Migrants from Africa and Asia crossing the Mediterranean in search of better work and living conditions are a manifestation of a deeper problem of the international system for which the industrialized countries, in Europe and beyond, share responsibility. Inequality in wealth and opportunities between the advanced and developing world is the engine for migration movements. No methods of combating smugglers, including the military ones, will stop these movements. Only a more equitable international economic system will be capable of stemming sudden and unpredictable flows.

The use of the term 'crisis' should not justify the adoption of exceptional measures that eat at the protection recognized for refugees under international refugee law and for migrants, as human beings, under international human rights law. 'Crises' are also opportunities. The 'crisis' in the Mediterranean region should be seized upon to reinforce protection and adapt it to present-day conditions and challenges. The regional sub-systems in the Middle East and in Europe, their peoples, and the international system as a whole will be the great beneficiaries of these reinforced protections and adaptations.

Tragedies have not completely disappeared and ships transporting migrants in distress occasionally fail to find a European port at which to moor. However, the flows of 2015–2016 have died out as a consequence of a combination of policies put in place by the EU, including its March 2016 deal with Turkey, increased capabilities of FRONTEX, the above-mentioned militarization of the fight against smuggling, and cooperation in border control with countries on the southern rim of the Mediterranean. The International Organization for Migration (IOM) reported that slightly fewer than half as many migrants reached Europe by sea in 2017 than in 2016: The IOM recorded 171,635 arrivals by boat in 2017, while the 2016 figure was 363,504.[1] The number of crossings continues to decrease. The UNHCR reported that the number of people crossing the Mediterranean by sea from Libya decreased by 74

---

1 Stephanie Nebehay, "Half as Many Migrants Landed in Europe in 2017 as 2016: IOM," Reuters, World News, January 5, 2018, https://www.reuters.com/article/us-europe-migrants-un/half-as-many-migrants-landed-in-europe-in-2017-as-2016-iom-idUSKBN1EU1KP

per cent in the first three months of 2018 compared to the same period in 2017.[2] The migration situation in the Mediterranean basin may be considered back to normal. In fact, migrant-transporting boats, such as those referred to at the beginning of this paragraph, should now be considered as a feature of normalcy in migration across the Mediterranean.

Return to normalcy is the reason the chapters in this issue of *Cairo Papers* go beyond the 'crisis' that was the subject of the 2017 symposium. Six chapters discuss various dimensions and aspects of migration in the Euro-Mediterranean region. They address the history of migration in the region, relations between Mediterranean countries of origin and their diasporas, the impact of interest groups on the formulation of migration policies in countries of destination, and the policies for integration of recent flows arriving in Europe.

Starting with history, Joseph John Viscomi and Angelos Dalachanis take up Italian migration in Egypt and the departure from Egypt of European migrants in the mid twentieth century. This is a reminder for those who have forgotten or are unaware of it that migration has long existed in the Mediterranean basin and that it was not always from south to north.

In "Between Italy and Egypt: Migrating Histories and Political Genealogies," Viscomi reviews successive waves of Italian migrants, from those arriving in Egypt under the Capitulation privileges through the flows, mainly from southern Italy, that were part of the period of great Italian emigration between 1861 and 1913. He describes the measures taken by the Italian authorities in the late nineteenth and early twentieth centuries to slow the pace of emigration to Egypt and emphasizes the high unemployment of Italians as a result of the 1907 international financial crisis. It is inevitable to think of the other side of the coin when, a century later, the 2008–2009 global financial crisis left many Egyptian and other migrant workers unemployed in Italy and elsewhere in Europe. Viscomi emphasizes the arrival in Egypt of un-contracted Italian migrant workers, in other words irregular migrants, for a whole decade, from 1905 to 1913. Importantly, he brings out the instrumentalization of the Italian community in Egypt by the fascist Italian regime in the 1920s and 1930s, which wanted to use it to counter British and French influences.

---

2 "Despite Drop in Numbers, Desperate Migrants to Europe Face Greater Perils," UN News, April 11, 2018, https://news.un.org/en/story/2018/04/1007031

In their discourse the fascists, like other Italian regimes before and after them, exalted the traditional friendship between Egypt and Italy as the basis for this migration. Foreign policy and economic interests were not dissociated from Italian migration, either positively or negatively. This is a clear indication of the existence of a Mediterranean migration system between Egypt and Italy.[3] However, although Italian migration to Egypt is similar in some ways to Egyptian migration to Italy a century later, Italian returnees find the comparison insulting. Italians had been invited to go to Egypt to contribute to its development and modernity. In contrast, in the words of a returnee interviewed by Viscomi, "Italy is now welcoming wretched populations and even thieves, bandits, and murderers." Elements of the fascist discourse apparently live on. These elements are found in the anti-immigrant and xenophobic ideologies of the present far-right and populist Italian parties.

As the title of his chapter indicates, "Kaleidoscopic Out-Migration: The Departure of Foreigners from Mid Twentieth Century Egypt," Angelos Dalachanis examines the departure of foreigners from Egypt in the mid twentieth century. Rather than 'migrants,' he uses the term 'foreigners,' in line with the category used in successive Egyptian censuses. Before advancing an explanation for the gradual departure of foreigners, he refers to the arrival in Egypt, in the course of the nineteenth century and the early decades of the twentieth, of migrants of multiple ethnic, religious, and national origins, including "non-skilled workers and destitute people." Dalachanis thus refutes claims that Europeans migrating to Egypt were only invited because they could contribute to its development and modernization. Joining Viscomi, he explains that foreigners benefited from the protection and broad privileges afforded them by the Capitulations. Dalachanis analyzes the decennial Egyptian population censuses between 1917 and 1960 to reveal the composition of foreign communities in Egypt and its evolution. He notes a peak in foreign presence in 1927 and a gradual decrease thereafter. For him, the departure of foreigners cannot be explained by Gamal Abdel Nasser's policies. It antedates him and should be understood instead as having been determined by two sets of factors. These are structural change and moments of crisis. The

---

3   The 'migration system' concept refers to migration as inserted in a network of relations that includes political issues, trade, and financial and cultural exchanges, in addition to the movement of people.

former relate to Egypt's state-building as it progressively achieved independence. The abolition of the Capitulations between 1937 and 1949, and with them the privileges foreigners enjoyed, was a structural change. Dealing in Arabic in business and in relations with the government, as decreed in the 1940s, is another expression of structural change. A third one was the need for the Egyptian state to leave room in its labor market for the increasingly educated Egyptians. This is the question of competition in labor markets, well known in labor migration studies. The Second World War, the Palestine war, the 1956 Suez war, decolonization, and the socialist laws of the early 1960s were the crises that either prompted or forced foreigners to leave Egypt. It is also interesting to note the competition between migrant communities that is apparent in labor migration analyses. When Italians left Egypt in large numbers in the late 1940s and early 1950s, the Greek community saw this as opening employment opportunities for its members. From the perspective of migration in the Mediterranean basin, it is significant to note that the largest communities were the Greek and Italian, well ahead of the British occupiers. Greeks and Italians were eager to emphasize that they had arrived in Egypt before the British and French, in order to dissociate themselves from the colonial powers. Other large Mediterranean communities were the Cypriots and Maltese. When the British had to leave after the Suez war, the Foreign Office was not alarmed by the fate of the Cypriots and Maltese, whose countries were associated with Britain. Dalachanis quotes one of its reports: "Both communities are closely assimilated to the local population and neither is likely to attract mob violence."

Leaping over decades and leaving history behind, Gerda Heck presents "Waiting in Izmir: Syrians in the Aegean Region after the 'EU–Turkey Deal.'" She argues that the lives of migrants and refugees are shaped by long periods of 'waiting,' not by mobility alone. Migrants and refugees wait for money in order to start moving, for smugglers, for residence permits, for decisions regarding their asylum applications, or for deportation. But they are not passive in waiting. They work, put down roots, and participate in reshaping the city space where they wait for the next decision affecting their lives or for the opportunity to put their plans into practice.

Heck has undertaken ethnographic research on Syrian refugees waiting in Basmane, Izmir. In her chapter she analyzes their agency during their period of waiting. Heck particularly examines the impact of the March 2016 EU–Turkey deal, which greatly reduced the number of attempts to cross the Aegean Sea to the nearer Greek islands and also increased waiting periods in Turkey. For Heck, the refugees may be victims of cheating by smugglers and exploitation by employers. But they also weigh the chances of success in crossing to the islands after the deal. They assess their personal conditions, their need to work, to earn income, and to educate their children. They make their decisions in the light of this assessment. For Heck, this shows that migrants and refugees are not mere objects of policy. They are subjects that affect policy on border control, in this case by the EU or Turkey. Migrants and refugees have agency. In addition to the compelling core of her argument, two passages of Heck's chapter are worth underlining. She refers to three protection statuses for non-Europeans in Turkey after 2013: the conditional protection status, the subsidiary protection status, and the temporary protection status. While these are useful new statuses, one wonders whether it would not have been simpler to lift the geographical and time limitations Turkey has set with respect to the application of the 1951 Convention Relating to the Status of Refugees and extend it to non-European asylum seekers. The second observation is about the 850,000 individuals who managed to cross the sea toward the Greek islands in 2015. Only half of these people were Syrian. This goes to show that the 2015–2016 'crisis' was not merely one of Syrian migrants and refugees. Its roots have to be uncovered and remedied.

Alexandra Parrs, in "Culturalized, Gendered, and Fractured Approaches to the Integration of Refugees in Brussels," discusses the two integration programs put in place by the Flemish and Walloon communities in Belgium. It may be safely assumed that these programs are intended for refugees similar to those interviewed by Heck if they succeed in reaching western Europe. Depending on certain conditions, in the Belgian capital migrants and refugees have to choose one of these two integration programs. The Flemish program emphasizes the cultural aspects of integration, and essentializes the cultures of both immigrants and the host community. It assumes the superiority of the host community's progressive Flemish culture and aims at the adoption by immigrants and refugees of its values and norms of outward and intimate behavior. Parrs wonders how a progressive culture can fail to admit diversity and difference in values and norms. She considers that the Flemish program is in line with the right-wing discourse of culturalization of citizenship and cultural integration. In contrast, the Walloon program of French-speaking Belgium, which only came into existence in 2003, a decade after its Flemish equivalent, emphasizes social rather than cultural dimensions of integration and does not refer to values and norms. She attributes this approach to the fact that Wallonia is not situated at the right of the political spectrum like Flanders. There are no far-right parties in Wallonia, which kept it from succumbing to populism. Parrs views the considerable difference between the two regional integration programs as indicative of the fracture of the Belgian political system. It may be added that the difference also eloquently expresses the importance of internal politics in constructing the discourse on migration and in formulating policies to govern it.

Gerasimos Tsourapas and Maysa Ayoub analyze emigration and refugee policies in five Mediterranean countries and in Germany. Under the title "Diaspora Politics in Illiberal Contexts: Authoritarianism and Cross-Border Mobility in the Modern Middle East," Tsourapas examines the emigration policies of Egypt, Jordan, Libya, Syria, and Turkey. He observes that a large amount of research has recently been done on policies of emigration and diaspora developed by liberal democracies, but that comparable policies put in place by autocracies and illiberal democracies are undertheorized. He conceptualizes such policies in three sets of measures: exit policy measures, overseas policy measures, and return policy measures. The first set is about facilitating or obstructing departure from the country in question. The second bears on links with diasporas in their countries of destination to monitor their behavior, to target families left behind, to extract financial resources from their members, to reinforce links with the homeland, and to extend voting rights to them. The third set of measures facilitates return, prevents it, or punishes returnees. It includes measures for authorizing or restricting access to dual citizenship, deprivation of nationality, forced extradition, and arrest upon return. Tsourapas's review clearly separates the countries whose policies he investigates into two groups. The first group, constituted by Libya and Syria, is suspicious of emigration and diasporas to the point of hostility. Under Muammar Gaddafi's regime, Libya restricted emigration, practiced "transnational repression" against diasporas, and resorted to assassination of its members. It arrested returnees upon return and prohibited dual citizenship. Syria, before the current civil strife, entered into bilateral labor agreements with a number of Arab countries, but the emigration process was cumbersome and exit visas were difficult to obtain. Unauthorized exit was punished. Like Libya, it also resorted to the assassination of opposition figures abroad, had a very restrictive policy on dual citizenship, and denied opponents passport renewal. In contrast, the second group of countries is positive toward emigration and diasporas. Egypt, Jordan, and Turkey considered that emigration helped to alleviate the employment question and contributed to development through the acquisition of skills and financial remittances. In slightly varied forms, the three countries entered into bilateral labor agreements with countries of destination and facilitated exit. They provided incentives for financial remittances, including by opening investment opportunities, and reinforced links with their diasporas. They facilitated return and established institutional frameworks aimed at supporting emigrants. In the cases of Egypt and Turkey, they allowed dual citizenship and extended voting rights to emigrants. Tsourapas admits that additional research is needed to understand policy variations between and within the two sets of countries and beyond.

Finally, Ayoub analyzes asylum policy-making in Germany. She reviews the roles that interest groups played during the 'crisis' in influencing policy from its initial open door to the later restrictive asylum legislation. After reviewing the numbers of Syrian asylum-seekers reaching Germany between 2012 and 2016, Ayoub reviews the history of the German resettlement policy, which only came into existence in 2008. She points out that the right to seek asylum is codified in the German Basic Law, and identifies the Asylum and the Residence Acts as the two most important immigration laws in Germany. For Ayoub the essence of refugees and immigrants and their intentions are social constructions. They are the factors that determine policies affecting them. She conceptualizes interest groups according to behavioral and organizational structure, and to narrow and broad scopes of interest, and then focuses on interest groups specifically concerned with migration, refugees, and asylum issues in Germany. Ayoub identifies three types of such groups: rights-based organizations, right-wing xenophobic and anti-immigrant groups, and hometown associations (HTA) set up by migrants.

Rights-based organizations critically monitor German human rights policy concerning refugees, engage in advocacy, make policy proposals, and campaign for admission or against deportation. Xenophobic anti-immigration groups have no organizational structures. They are made up of neo-Nazis and of unemployed and socially marginalized youth, but also attract individuals with center-right leanings. Xenophobic anti-immigration groups existed before the refugee influx of 2012–2016 but seized the opportunity to mobilize in favor of right-wing policies. Ayoub particularly examines the Patriotic Europeans against the Islamization of the Occident (PEGIDA). PEGIDA's strategy includes demonstrations, portraying the other as a threat, and demonizing him/her. Ayoub points out the ambivalent attitudes of policymakers toward PEGIDA's arguments and notes a turn to the right of participants in its demonstrations. Syrian HTAs existed before the Syrian conflict but have increased since 2011. Some focus their activities in Syria and others in Germany. Among the latter, activities extend from fostering integration in Germany to the promotion of cultural events and community development. By providing a space for discussions, HTAs allow for the participation of their members in influencing policy in the host country. Ayoub finally considers that the increasingly restrictive German asylum policy is an indication of the influence of the anti-refugee movement.

This issue of *Cairo Papers* takes up migration and refugees in the Euro-Mediterranean region in different periods in the last two centuries. It addresses migration and refugees from Europe in the southern rim of the Mediterranean and from this southern as well as eastern rims in Europe. The disciplines of history, sociology, anthropology, and political science have been mobilized to undertake the research its chapters embody. The issue will no doubt be a valuable contribution to scholarship on Euro-Mediterranean migration and refugees.

**References**

Awad, Ibrahim. 2013. "The Arab Spring and Population Movements in the Mediterranean Region." In *Regional Dynamics in the Mediterranean and Prospects for Transatlantic Cooperation*, 13–24. Mediterranean Paper Series, no. 22. The German Marshall Fund of the United States and Istituto Affari Internazionali (IAI).

CHAPTER 2

# Between Italy and Egypt: Migrating Histories and Political Genealogies

*Joseph John Viscomi*

During the early summer of 2013, in a town in al-Qalyubiya, I met Ashraf al-Batawi,[1] who had worked and lived in northern Italy intermittently since the 1980s. Although he had decided not to renew his residency visa, and thus relinquished his right to enter Italy as a documented immigrant, his younger brother had only recently arrived there in search of work. Ashraf anticipated growing hostility toward foreigners in Italy as work opportunities declined after the 2008 economic recession. For his brother, however, the promise of migration outweighed its potential hardship.

Following Ashraf's advice, I traveled to Italy to speak further with his brother and the extended community of Egyptian migrant workers living in northern Italy. Once in Treviglio, where roughly 18% of the town's immigrant population comes from Egypt,[2] I went to the local pizzeria, Le piramidi, to await his brother. There, I spoke with Sa'id, who prepared pizza for a steady flow of Italian customers while a group of unemployed and underemployed Egyptians lingered outside. At one point, Sa'id paused and said:

> *This isn't the first time a foreigner (*agnabi*) has come in here speaking Arabic . . . once, this old Italian woman began speaking to me in Egyptian Arabic (*bi-l-masri*). . . . I was surprised because she was speaking* skandrani, *with an Alexandrian accent, which is where I*

---
1 All names have been changed.
2 http://www.tuttitalia.it/lombardia/85-treviglio/statistiche/cittadini-stranieri-2016/

*am from. . . . I asked her how she learned the language and she laughed at me, saying "I was born there! Egypt is also my country!"*

"You know," he continued, "once there were thousands of Italians in Egypt!" Ashraf's brother eventually arrived and I left, but Sa'id's story haunted me throughout the preliminary months of my research on Egyptian migrant workers in Italy.

In this chapter, I will demonstrate how various iterations of the presence of Italians in Egypt have been mobilized in order to reinforce political genealogies in the mid twentieth century. As I spent more time with Egyptians in Lombardia—the region that is home to Italy's largest concentration of immigrants and also a stronghold of the right-wing political party, la Lega Nord, which has increasingly espoused a vehemently anti-immigration rhetoric (Richardson and Colombo 2013)—I found that Egyptian migrants frequently and strategically referred to the past presence of Italians in Egypt. In contextualizing their own presence in Italy within this broader historical framework, they consciously used history to counter the growing animosity they experienced in the present. As we will see, however, histories of the Italian community in Egypt have operated to configure moral hierarchies in the Mediterranean since the community's establishment. The historical constellations conjured in this tale, then, importantly help us to understand a set of relations and geopolitical processes that continue to influence and affect contemporary understandings of Mediterranean crossings.

## Arrivals

The *longue durée* of the Italian presence in Egypt is complicated at once by the lack of historiographical material available on the community and by the narratives that do exist concerning the community's history (which are predominantly nostalgic accounts written by elite members of the community itself or by its many visitors) (Santorelli 1894; Balboni 1906; Dori 1959; Biolato 2008; Viviani 2014).

Italian settlement in Egypt was encouraged, among other factors, by two main contingencies. The first was the existence of the Capitulations (known in Arabic as *al-imtiyazat*), a series of antiquated bilateral treaties between the Ottoman Porte and European powers dating back to the sixteenth century. These treaties effectively created enclaves of legal extraterritoriality for some European subjects. These treaties continued to function—albeit in modified forms—into much of the late-Ottoman and colonial Mediterranean, and remained active in Egypt as late as 1937.

The second factor that encouraged Italian settlement in Egypt was the large number of professionals, merchants, and workers who had arrived from the Italian peninsula during and after the reign of Mehmet Ali Pasha (1805–1848). Long before the unification of the Italian state, some of these "Italians" had been merchants who crossed the Mediterranean since the time of the Maritime Republics, others were individuals who participated in Napoleon's campaign in Egypt (1798–1801) and stayed in some capacity, and still others were political elites who escaped turmoil in the Italian peninsula during the Risorgimento (1815–1871).

Until Italian unification (1861), these individuals lived in Egypt under the authority of their respective consuls (Tuscan, Sardinian, and Venetian, mainly, but some also held French or British protection). After 1864 the "Italian" consulates were consolidated under one national consul.[3] Then, following the British occupation of Egypt in 1882, an event more or less coterminous with Italy's period of great emigration (1861–1913), a new influx of immigrants crossed Egypt's borders. This new wave came mostly from Italy's south, but another large group was constituted by Italian Sephardic *protetti* (protected subjects)—Ottoman Jews who held a limited form of Italian nationality. Between the outbreak of the Italo-Turkish war in 1911 (which saw Italian residents expelled from Beirut, Damascus, Aleppo, and Jerusalem[4]) and later Greek–Turkish conflicts, many of Italy's *protetti* fled to safer harbors in Alexandria where they would continue to live under the protection of the Italian consul. Their numbers are not easily discernible, and sometimes in the literature they encompass a population commonly denominated as "levantines" (*levantini*, which may or may not include non-Jewish Italians). We do know, however, from Egyptian census data that the population of Italian Jews registered in Egypt grew from 4,348

---

3 The process took several years.
4 When the war broke out, Italians were threatened with expulsion and the Italian state was threatened with the prospect of having to assist a large community of refugees. Although many returned to these cities, others took the departure as a sign of continued hardship and settled elsewhere. Childs 1997:84–85.

in 1897 to 6,629 in 1917, and a large portion of this growth was likely the result of the influx of Italian *protetti* (Amicucci 2000:84).

Almost immediately following British occupation in 1882, Anglo-Egyptian authorities attempted to limit immigration due to growing tensions between ethnic and national groups (Owen 1981:134). They particularly feared the consequences of the growth of an Italian "proletarian immigration" because it competed in a labor market with Egyptian laborers and tradesmen.[5] As early as 1899 the Emigration Office in Italy (a division of the Ministry of Foreign Affairs) took measures to slow the pace of immigration by publicizing the "destitute conditions" encountered by Italian workers upon their arrival in Egypt.[6] British authorities cautioned Italian police to enforce stricter controls on Italian ports of emigration. Despite these attempts, by 1907 the population of Italian residents had grown to 34,926. The financial crisis that same year—which collapsed the construction market in Alexandria and Cairo—left many Italians unemployed (Hansen 1985:356).

The Emigration Office in Rome noted that authorities in Egypt continued to complain that "the excessive crowding in Egypt of temporary Italian workers unable to find work [was becoming] disruptive to public order."[7] "Public order" had been the rallying cry during previous attempts to control emigration at the port of Naples. In 1905 and 1906, several complaints were sent from the Italian consulate in Port Said, decrying the continuous arrival of un-contracted workers, especially from the Italian south.[8] A similar statement circulated in 1913, during the peak year of Italian emigration, reiterating the foreign minister's request that the Emigration Office not release passports to men without contracts intending to travel to Egypt (Choate 2008:26). Describing all

---

5  Hansen 1985; Chalcraft 2005:127. For an excellent discussion of competition between Egyptian and foreign workers in Egypt during this period, see Lockman 1993; Beinin and Lockman 1987.

6  Ministero degli Affari Esteri, "Notizie concernenti l'emigrazione italiana—Emigrazione in Egitto," *Bollettino del Ministero degli Affari Esteri* (August–September, 1899).

7  Archivio di Stato Napoli (ASN), Questura di Napoli, Gabinetto-Seconda Serie (1902–1971), Massime, b.54, f.1080 "Egitto-Emigrazione (1898–1937)," *Gazzetta Ufficiale del Regno d'Italia*, October 7, 1908.

8  ASN, Questura di Napoli, Gabinetto-Seconda Serie (1902–1971), Massime, b.54, f.1080 "Egitto-Emigrazione (1898–1937)," handwritten notes anonymously signed by *Consolato italiano a P.S.* 1905 and 1906.

economic activity in Alexandria and Cairo as "paralyzed," it added that with the proliferation of unregulated prostitution, under no circumstances should passports be issued to women traveling alone.[9]

In a series of telegrams from 1915, the British tried to restrict working-class immigration by requiring potential emigrants to consult the British consulate in Naples prior to their departure. In 1917, Italians in Egypt numbered 40,198 persons. Still, no law explicitly regulated immigration to Egypt. A British decree passed in 1920 required individuals disembarking in Egypt to hold a British visa, but it was dissolved in 1922 with England's unilateral declaration of Egypt's independence (Petricioli 2007:73). By 1927, Italian residents had grown to number 52,462. One decade later, when Italians constituted roughly 25 percent of the 186,515 foreign residents in Egypt (a community second in size only to Greeks), unemployment among them was widespread. A telegram from one British administrator in Egypt to the prefect in Naples stated: "Requests for manual workers are easily covered by the unemployed who are already present [here] . . . those intending to depart in search of work should be discouraged."

## Becoming Italians of Egypt

Beginning in the late 1920s, and after its consolidation of power in Rome, the Fascist regime hoped to expand its influence over the Italians dispersed throughout the world. Through political propaganda and financial support of nationalist and cultural institutions, the regime attempted to create islands of "nationalist" Italian communities throughout the Mediterranean. In addition to Italy's territorial occupation of Libya and Greece, these communities were part of the fascist vision to render the sea "an Italian lake." Such efforts received greater attention in Egypt, as the Fascist regime viewed emigrant Italians there as a strategic "asset"—a possible community—that could serve to undermine French and British hegemony in the Mediterranean.

Thus, while investing heavily in cultural institutions to centralize the population of Italian residents, the regime also poured its resources into

---

9 ASN, Questura di Napoli, Gabinetto-Seconda Serie (1902–1971), Massime, b.54, f.1080 "Egitto-Emigrazione (1898–1937)," Ufficio dell'emigrazione per i confini di terra, February 13, 1913. For more on the role of Italian and other foreign women in the history of prostitution in colonial Egypt, see Biancani 2015; Gobbi 2011.

anti-British movements among Egyptian nationalists. From Rome, the Fascist government bribed journalists in Egypt representing newspapers published in Arabic, French, Greek, and English.[10] Radio Bari, the first internationally broadcast Arabic-language radio station, was one of Italy's most powerful weapons in this endeavor. "Its cultural programs presented Italy as a 'friendly nation' to its Arabic-speaking audience by omitting news of the violence and strife in the Italian colonies in Libya and Ethiopia" (Grange 1974:171). Sixty percent of the broadcasts by Radio Bari were considered "cultural programs" that covered historical encounters between Italians and Muslims.[11] This was part of the political project of mythologizing the timeless links between Italy and the Arab or Islamic world. Rather than engendering sympathy for the Italian regime, however, Radio Bari was deemed successful because of its ability to incite Egyptian and Arab nationalists against British and French hegemony in the Mediterranean.[12]

Seeking to erode the British from within, the presence of Italian residents in Egypt proved strategically important—they became the node at which geopolitical histories of "friendship" (*amicizia*) intersected between Italy and Egypt. The consequences of the 1930s are best condensed in the work of Italian schoolteacher and historian Angelo Sammarco, a confidant of King Fuad. Entrusting Sammarco with the Egyptian royal family's archives, Fuad assigned to him the task of reconstructing the history of modern Egypt. On the occasion of the Italian king's visit to Egypt in 1933, Sammarco published an article in *Al-Ahram*, celebrating an ageless "friendship" between the two nations

---

10 Archivio Storico-Diplomatico Ministero degli Affari Esteri (MAE) Affari Politici (AP) Egitto 1931–45 B16, "Pretesa propaganda italiana in Egitto."

11 Although the substance of these broadcasts is not readily available, one of the authors, Said Sciartuni, published a series of articles around the same time that reflect what was aired on Radio Bari. See, for example, Sciartuni 1939; 1937. For a broader analysis of Radio Bari and its impact and role in fascist propaganda, see Marzano 2015.

12 Grange 1974:174, 185. It should also be noted that the Italian minister in Egypt reported that British authorities expressed outright discontent regarding the broadcasts of Radio Bari. See MAE, APE (1931–45) Egitto, B.16, fasc. "Pretesa propaganda italiana in Egitto." Philip Shukry Khoury has shown that the strength of Italian propaganda emanating from Egypt was more than a simple "menace." It caused both the British and the French great worry in the eastern Mediterranean. See Khoury 1987:494, 509, 514.

and peoples.[13] Then, several years later, Sammarco was summoned by the Italian Ministero della Cultura Popolare—Italy's propaganda ministry—to organize the translation and distribution of anti-British texts, ensuring their circulation in both English and Arabic. Until 1940, Sammarco, alongside other prominent members of the Italian Fascist Party in Egypt, promulgated the notion that since Mehmet Ali's reforms—indeed, long before Italian unification—the Italian "colony"[14] and its "timeless friendship to Egypt" helped deliver Egypt to modernity through a series of close partnerships.

The stories they employed to substantiate this narrative hailed instead from the generation that preceded the mass immigration of Italians into Egypt after 1882.[15] In this imaginary, Sammarco and other fascist intellectuals knotted the politics of community-making to the dynamics of competing Mediterranean imperialisms. This approach was measurably successful, in part due to the fact that the extraterritorial conditions set by the Capitulations facilitated a more direct extension of the Italian state over its subjects in Egypt—one that was relatively free of British or Egyptian interference.

What was once described by observers as a dispersed and fragmented group of Italian subjects, representing a broad political spectrum—in the context of the same liberal Mediterranean that witnessed the spread of radicalism until the outbreak of the First World War (Khury-Makdisi 2010)—had morphed by the late 1930s into a tightly integrated national community.[16] It was one that ardently participated in state-led initiatives and, when called upon to donate for Italian imperialist causes (for example, in 1935 during Italy's Ethiopia campaign), donated more per capita than Italians in metropolitan Italy.

The observations of a contemporary British political scientist are interesting here, for they trace this trajectory. Elizabeth Monroe's observations are worth quoting at length.

---

13 Angelo Sammarco, "al-Tuliyyan fi Misr," *Al-Ahram*, February 19, 1933.
14 *Colonie*, in this sense, simply means 'community.'
15 L. A. Balboni's three-volume study, published in 1906, already speaks of the Italians of Egypt as a community of the past (Balboni 1906).
16 Several British accounts detail the same transformation. See Monroe 1938; Martelli 1938.

> *At first sight [the Italian emigrant] looked unprepossessing, for the Italian emigrant was hardly an inspiring type.... He forgot his Italian origin, and accepted wages lower than did other westerners. In fact, he sank to the depths of poverty in everything but the size of his family.... Such was the creature whom Fascism set out to waken to a sense of national pride, and it did so by the simple method of making him feel important. It taught him to fly an Italian flag, and to display pictures of his King and Duce. It turned his ragamuffin children into spick-and-span Ballilas, complete with black shirt, blue neckerchief, and toy gun. It improved his bastard Italian, and built him bigger schools and better hospitals; it provided clubs and night schools and aftercare; it offered free holidays in Italy to his schoolboy and student sons, and it ran excursions from Cairo to the Suez Canal in order that he might see Italian troopships go by.... It has achieved a great work for Italy. The communities still live in slums, for standards of living cannot be raised in a day and the older generation, which is conservative, has not appreciably changed its habits; but elsewhere a miracle has been worked. Their sons and grandsons are a new breed, radiating not only national loyalty but self-respect.* (Monroe 1938:196–197)

The transformation of the Italian community was so extensive that, within days of Italy's entry into the Second World War in June 1940, Anglo-Egyptian authorities repatriated Italian diplomats, closed all Italian institutions, froze Italian bank accounts, and made it illegal for others to sign contracts with Italians. Egyptian police also began to arrest and imprison what would amount to over 5,000 Italian civilians in Fayed, a militarized zone in Egypt's eastern desert.[17] This was a compromise, as the British hoped to imprison as many as 12,000. Initially the plan received limited support from Ali Maher's Egyptian government, but the British "pressured" King Faruq to change his cabinet. With the young king's power at stake, he quickly followed suit.[18]

---

17 This is also known as the Tombak Plan, and had been conceived earlier in the 1930s when the Italian campaign to invade Ethiopia had fostered greater tensions between the Italian and British governments.

18 Eric Schewe has written an excellent dissertation that deals with some of the political battles between the Egyptian government and the British authorities during the Second World War: Schewe 2014.

The experiences during the Second World War formed tight boundaries around the community. Any relief that came with the end of the war and the release from Fayed was short-lived. It quickly became apparent to many how little postwar Egypt—and the broader landscape of postwar Mediterranean politics—would resemble the recent past. After over four years of internment and unemployment, freed Italians were, as described by one delegate from the Holy See, "living in complete destitution."

By the late 1940s, when diplomatic ties between Italy and Egypt were restored and some of the restrictions that had been placed upon Italians were lifted, Egypt's future markedly diverged from its past. Italian residents had few resources to carve out a present in Egypt. The conditions that had facilitated the emergence of an Italian community quickly faded. The 1937 Montreux Convention to abolish the Capitulations set a 12-year transitional period during which the Egypt government would gain increasing sovereignty over its territorial borders. This process would formally annul the privileges previously conferred on foreigners. In 1947, the Egyptian government enacted the Company Law to further "Egyptianize" the workforce, thus establishing strict quotas for foreign employment (Karanasou 1992).

## Fading Horizons

As the pace of Egypt's decolonization accelerated, departure became an imminent reality for Italians. Within these historical trajectories, many Italian residents envisioned a resolution in "repatriation." Contrary to much of the historiographical literature, which depicts departure as almost inextricably linked to Nasser's post-1956 policies of nationalization (*ta'mim*), "repatriation" had informed discourses on Italian futures in Egypt at least since 1919.

This detail conjures up hierarchies of a colonial Mediterranean that persisted despite claims of solidarity and "friendship" across national boundaries. The propaganda of the Fascist government in Rome had so effectively intertwined the genealogy of Italy's emigrants in Egypt to its nationalist "prestige" that "repatriation"—the official relocation of the community from Egypt to Italy, a literal "return to *Patria*"—surfaced as the most logical "return" for the community.

After the collapse of Mussolini's regime, however, the Italian state was averse to accommodating the very subjects that the Fascist regime lauded as emblematic of Italy's "prestige" abroad. On one hand, the influx of repatriates without material or familial connections in Italy would place a heavy burden on the country's delicate postwar economy. The Italian state thus avoided repatriation, instead seeking concessions that would either keep Italians in Egypt or send them on to new destinations. Although Egyptian citizenship was offered to foreign residents in Egypt (around 1948), few took advantage of the option and those who did often found their requests denied (estimates of over 66 percent).[19] On the other hand, the community's nostalgia for the Fascist regime threatened to disrupt the fragile political balance in the new Italian republic. Italians in Egypt had been largely cut off from the direct impacts of fascism suffered by many in metropolitan Italy, and emergent postwar politicians—particularly in the first years of the Italian republic—feared that repatriating these Italians would sway the political field toward the right. Indeed, members of the neo-fascist Italian Social Movement (Movimento Sociale Italiano) called upon the postwar government to provide resources for this population of "displaced" Italians who had "served" the nation abroad.

For the Italian residents themselves, emigration from Egypt was often the sole alternative to increasing unemployment. It was estimated that the decline in the population was around "20 to 25 percent." Although official statistics showed that some 1,086 families had left Egypt since 1949, the numbers were likely much higher.[20] Only 655 "definitive departures" were registered between 1946 and 1951. However, during this period, many left without registering precisely because a definitive departure signified abandoning one's rights to residency if circumstances proved uninviting elsewhere. Many hoped that this was something a sponsored emigration would alleviate. Over 30% of the population was officially unemployed. Apart from the hundreds of workers laid off as a result of the new company laws, a 1954 consular

---

19 MAE AP Egitto 1951 B703, Appunto acquisto della cittadinanza egiziana, October 30, 1950. I have yet to see precise numbers on this, but I do know that around 800 requests total (from all foreigners) were received by the Egyptian government.

20 The departures of part of a family or temporary departure of individuals who did not register their departure so as not to relinquish residency are likely excluded from these estimates. Instead, these numbers should reflect only the number of "official" departures, which means those that were somehow arranged or conducted through the consulates.

report noted the impending problem of the hundreds of unemployed youth seeking their first jobs. There were 1,053 families receiving welfare support. Subsidies took the form of monthly or biweekly distributions of one-half to two Egyptian pounds per family, depending on need.[21] A total of LE 1,373,710 in aid was distributed over the course of 1954. Once the elite structure on which much of the community relied, so many of the *protetti*—the definition of their citizenship status still ambiguous, especially with the end of a model of imperialism that sought to profit from their presence in the Levant—requested passport renewals for departure that the Italian Foreign Ministry, the consulates in Egypt, and Italian authorities in Turkey compiled a partial list of the families that had arrived as *protetti* from Ottoman territories at the beginning of the century to determine whether the Italian government was legally responsible for them.[22]

In the same consular report, the consul draws attention to an important factor which, he claimed, provided definitive evidence that the Italians of Egypt would be unable to integrate into metropolitan Italy. He wrote:

> *Without family ties, which are especially important for the reinsertion in the national life of those individuals who repatriate even after a few years' absence, accustomed to living conditions totally different from those in Italy, speaking a language deformed by the long presence in the Near East to the point of making it perceptibly different from what we speak, these compatriots (*connazionali*), once repatriated, would end up feeling foreign in the country of which they have nationality, and might even regret what they had left [behind], notwithstanding the life of restrictions and humiliation that they were constrained to live.*[23]

The historical and political conditions that had shaped the Italian community, he claimed, had rendered the community coherent in such a way that it could no longer conform to the present circumstances. This "abnormal" situation, however, could not be prolonged, argued

---

21 This data comes from the consultation of the *registri* archives at the now defunct Consolato Generale in Alexandria and the current Cancelleria Consolare in Cairo, where each receipt of received payment is placed in the individual family folders.
22 MAE AP Egitto 1955 B1006 "Rapporto Consolare 1954," Alexandria, June 30, 1955.
23 MAE AP Egitto 1955 B1006 "Rapporto Consolare 1954," Alexandria, June 30, 1955.

the consul. Enduring circumstances had forced the Italian residents to "panhandle" (*elemosinare*) from the consular offices and the locally based Italian Charity Organization (*Società italiana di beneficenza*). Many awaited "any initiative" that might bring stability to their lives—even confronting the risks of another emigration. In the 1954 report, the consul added that if there had been a moment to encourage naturalization, it had long passed, and thus action needed to be taken

> *to exit from this paralysis that could be dangerous to the morale of our nationals, who naturally associate the memory of a period of exceptional prosperity at the time of the Capitulations with the particular prestige promised to Italian communities abroad by the authoritarian regime of the Ventennio [the "twenty years," as the fascist period is often remembered in Italian historiography].*[24]

Until that moment, departures had been largely independent choices of individuals and families who were finally able to settle elsewhere. The consul, however, began to see the need for a comprehensive state-level policy that would address the question. He wrote: "I see no other alternative than massive repatriation unless *a series of windfalls opens new employment possibilities in other countries for the chronically unemployed of Alexandria.*"[25]

## Becoming Refugees

The limitations that had grown to characterize the collective life of the community put the entire population at risk of impoverishment. The consul's report had excluded both the integration of the Italians of Egypt into postwar Italian society and the possibility that the community could remain in Egypt without any significant legal or political return to past policy. Within this framework, emigration was the only solution. When it became clear to Italians in Egypt that the Italian state would not provide for a collective repatriation, and feeling neglected by the Italian republic, many chose emigration to Australia, South America, and elsewhere in Europe. In 1950 and 1951, reports estimated that as many as 6,000 Italian families had left Egypt since the end of the war, searching in "other locales the security of a future more prosperous and

---

24 MAE AP Egitto 1955 B1006 "Rapporto Consolare 1954," Alexandria, June 30, 1955.
25 MAE AP Egitto 1955 B1006 "Rapporto Consolare 1954," Alexandria, June 30, 1955.

serene."[26] One Italian resident of Port Said wrote of an "exodus" from the Suez Canal Zone: "Those who can get out, do!"[27]

In 1953, following the Free Officers coup d'état and the declaration of Egypt's republic, the dethroned King Faruq departed for Italy. Negotiating Faruq's exile, the political leaders in Italy and Egypt yet again invoked a timeless "friendship" encapsulated in the "hospitality" Egypt extended to Italian residents and to their own exiled king, Vittorio Emanuele III, who had left Italy for Alexandria, where he remained entombed until December 2017. Both parties emphasized that the exchange of dethroned kings would be a vital demonstration of their close relations and would strengthen their future ties.[28]

Just after the Free Officers declared a three-year transitional period of martial law in January 1953, the Italian Ministry of Defense sent Randolfo Pacciardi to visit President Muhammad Naguib in Egypt. The revelation brought contempt from the British.[29] The visit was intended to solidify these burgeoning ties and unite Italy and Egypt in a new politics aligned on the "defense of the Mediterranean." However, the scope of the visit included other aspects, as Pacciardi was to inquire about Naguib's personal insights on the internal situation and on the military regime's plans for Egypt's future and for that of the larger network of Middle Eastern and North African countries (it is important to note here that Pacciardi was a major proponent of Italy's participation in NATO). In 1954, these exchanges culminated in the acquisition of rights by Enrico Mattei, the Italian oil tycoon, to explore for oil in Egypt's deserts. The partnership between Ente Nazionale Idrocarburi (ENI) and the Egyptian regime was envisioned by the Italian state as a continuation of the "traditional spirit of friendship" between the two countries and marked a victory for the Italian company, which had seen previous efforts to procure accords stifled by Americans in Iran.[30]

---

26 G.P.d.F. "Il passato e il presente degli italiani in Egitto," *Italiani nel Mondo*, February 25, 1951.
27 R. Giani, "Declino a Porto Said della collettività italiana," *Italiani nel Mondo*, January 25, 1951.
28 MAE AP Egitto 1953 B870.
29 MAE AP Egitto 1953 B871 Appunto January 30, 1953.
30 MAE AP Egitto 1956 B1048 "oleodotto Suez-Cairo," July 25, 1956; CEA, *Cronaca*, July 28, 1956; Corduas 2006; Votaw 1964; Frankel 1966.

Importantly, ENI was also representative of the new kind of partnership between the countries, one built on high-level industrial agreements that did not mirror the interests of the on-the-ground realities of Italian residents. Several years later, during the events of 1956 when Italians were departing in haste, Italian diplomats implored Mattei to remain in the country. His presence, they contended, was the last trace of that political "friendship" which they feared was being extinguished by the departure en masse of Italian residents.

At least 3,000 Italian families left between November 1956 and January 1957 (some reports count as many as 10,000 departures). Italian residents in the Canal Zone, Alexandria, and Cairo flooded consular offices with requests for collective or subsidized repatriation, as many could not afford the cost of the journey. The Italian government, however, continued to refuse (or strategically delayed) taking collective action out of fear that it would convey a loss of faith in Nasser's regime and thus compromise political relations. Part of the risk of a collective repatriation, as understood by the Italian authorities, was the perceived damage it would cause to the deals diplomats had brokered between Nasser and the Italian industrialists.

From the late 1950s into the 1960s, when the Italian community in Egypt had all but ceased to exist, Italian foreign policy was characterized by what has been called an "Arab" or "Mediterranean" politics (Onelli 2013; Pizzigallo 2008). This position was founded around the myth of the "historic" community of Italian residents, their contribution to Egypt's modernity, and the institutional and infrastructural marks left on the Egyptian landscape. But on Italian shores another story was emerging.

In Italy, Italians who had departed Egypt were entitled to temporary housing as "refugees," and were encouraged to emigrate elsewhere. Conditions in the refugee camps—many of which were converted military barracks or former prisoner-of-war camps—deteriorated as official policy for addressing the influx of Italian "repatriates" and "refugees" was consistently stymied by political debate. An independent group emerged—the National Committee of Italians of Egypt, CoNIE—which was made up of displaced Italians from Egypt who sought to ease the "re-entry" in Italy and to protect the interests of "those who, with great sacrifice, had worked [for Italy] in Africa." The Italian government cautioned municipalities throughout Italian cities of the need to suppress organizations such as CoNIE, which could threaten relations with Egypt. At the same time, the Italian government strengthened ties with Egypt on the basis of this same, thinning community.[31] Indeed, to this day, the Italians of Egypt largely fault not Nasser for their circumstances, but the postwar Italian government.

## On the Politics of Origin

Although the Italian community's origins are not easily identifiable, in many ways the terms of its departure are. Indeed, the historical conjunctures that brought the departure of the Italians from Egypt are precisely those trajectories responsible, I contend, for the coherence—and persistence—of this particular community. Furthermore, the entanglements that shaped the Italian community in and beyond Egypt suggest a geopolitical history that ties contemporary migration to the historical processes of decolonizing the Mediterranean.

Once in Italy, the Italians of Egypt reconfigured new lives (and new futures). Repatriates often sought to distinguish their own experiences from those of the other migrants—internal migrants from the Italian south, Italian emigrants elsewhere, and immigrants in today's Italy. The departure/arrival relation—signifying the definitive spatial displacement from Egypt to Italy—compelled many Italians of Egypt to confront new realities in postwar Italy. In an interview with G.A., an Italian who had departed Egypt in the early 1950s, he described himself as "a strong Italian (*un italiano forte*)." He had driven from the Veneto region in the north to Rome to attend a meeting of Associazione Italiani d'Egitto (AIDE), a group that stems from the original CoNIE. G.A. remembered his initial impressions of Italy. Putting the collective experience of the Italians of Egypt in context, he said:

> *The Italians [of Italy,* gl'italiani d'Italia*] had another input . . . other ideologies . . . after the war they took that other one [he generally conflates a leftist and communist position here] . . . and . . . they said to us, "But you Italians colonized," to which I responded, "Go read your history!" and you see that's what we're doing here with AIDE. . . . Yeah, it's true, some among us brought over a relative [to Egypt], but we went there invited (*noi siamo andati lí chiamati*).*

---

31 MAE DGAP 1948-60 Uff.III B148, MAE to PCM, November 30, 1957.

To G.A., the Italians of Egypt, when they were in Egypt, did not represent a community of immigrants. They did not arrive "with a suitcase in hand," he continued, but instead had been "invited" to assist in Egypt's development since the mid nineteenth century. This exceptionality, he claimed, went unrecognized upon their arrival in Italy—and was interpreted in "other" ways, as he alluded to the anti-colonialist sentiments of the Italian left during the postwar years. Italians of Egypt, he recalled, were received as colonizers. "[Italians of Italy] did not understand our history," he argued. Due to similar encounters, many years passed before G.A. befriended Italians (of Italy). Today, he admitted, apologetically, "we're a little more Italianized (*siamo un po' più italianizzati*)."

This constellation of migration, politics, and history was not one merely gazing toward the past, but one that continuously extended into the present. As one interview with a member of AIDE concluded, G.S. compared his experience and that of other Italians of Egypt to an Italian (of Italy) of his own generation. He noted that—notwithstanding the technical education he and his peers received at the Don Bosco Institute—the Italians of Italy (*gl'italiani d'Italia*) were "three levels lower" (*tre livelli più giù*) than they. On Italian emigrants elsewhere, he thought aloud, "In Canada? In Brazil? What did the Italians do? In America ... there they did more damage than good ... while we ... we did (*mentre noi ... abbiamo fatto*)!" As a final punctuation, G.S. added, "I'm proud to be Italian, but I'm prouder to be an Italian of Egypt."[32]

Others placed their own experiences arriving in postwar Italy in relation to those of contemporary migrants and refugees in Italy.

> *It was really disgusting how and where the Italians of Egypt were received [in Italy] ... they were more Italian than the Italians in Italy. ... It certainly wasn't the way in which Italy is now welcoming wretched populations (*popolazioni disgraziate*) and even thieves, bandits, and murders.*

P.P., an Italian from Egypt who departed with her mother and sister in the midst of the 1956 war, denounced a political speech in which the prime minister at the time, Matteo Renzi, reminded his audience of the

---

32 "*Sono fiero di essere italiano, ma sono più fiero di essere italiano d'Egitto!*"

country's history of emigration, in light of xenophobic responses to the influx of migrants and refugees in Italy:

> *What permits [Renzi] to equate today's immigrants with our descendants? . . . They worked hard, some earned more than others, sure, but they contributed to the growth of the countries in which they arrived. . . . Look how we left Egypt. . . . Shame on him!*

P.P. condemned Renzi's interpretation of history, arguing that the "arrogance of [today's] clandestine migrants" failed to compare to the work ethic of Italian emigrants, especially those who had lived in Egypt. At the different moments in this story, the conjured past traces a constellation of histories through time, and is employed to position historical figures within a moral hierarchy of Mediterranean belonging. Ironically, the same political genealogies that are drawn upon to position the Italians of Egypt as marginalized are presented by Egyptian migrants in order to navigate the growing anti-immigration sentiment in contemporary Italy. The Mediterranean in which these histories continue to migrate, then, is one in which the processes of decolonization and contemporary migration are deeply intertwined.

## References

Amicucci, Davide. 2000. "La comunità italiana in Egitto attraverso i censimenti dal 1882 al 1947." In Paolo Branca, ed. *Tradizione e modernizzazione in Egitto 1798–1998*, 81–94. Milan: Angeli.

Balboni, L. A. 1906. *Gl'Italiani nella civiltà egiziana del secolo XIX*. Alexandria: Tipo-lit. V. Penasson.

Beinin, Joel, and Zachary Lockman. 1987. *Workers on the Nile: Nationalism, Communism, Islam and the Egyptian Working Class, 1882–1954*. Princeton: Princeton University Press.

Biancani, Francesca. 2015. "International Migration and Sex Work in Early Twentieth-Century Cairo." In Liat Kozma, Cyrus Schayegh, and Avner Wishnitzer, eds. *A Global Middle East: Mobility, Materiality and Culture in the Modern Age, 1880–1940*, 109–133. London: I.B. Tauris.

Biolato, Luca D. 2008. "Gli italiani fondatori delle moderne poste egiziane," *Oriente Moderno*, 88: 151–197.

Chalcraft, John T. 2005. *The Striking Cabbies of Cairo and Other Stories: Crafts and Guilds in Egypt, 1863–1914*. Albany: State University of New York Press.

Childs, Timothy Winston. 1990. *Italo-Turkish Diplomacy and the War over Libya: 1911–1912*. Leiden: Brill.

Choate, Mark I. 2008. *Emigrant Nation: The Making of Italy Abroad*. Cambridge: Harvard University Press.

Corduas, Claudio. 2006. *Impresa e cultura: L'utopia di ENI*. Milan: B. Mondadori.

Dori, Luigi. 1959. "Italiani in Africa: Tipografi e giornalisti italiani in Egitto," *Africa: Rivista trimestrale di studi e documentazione dell'Istituto italiani per l'Africa e l'Oriente*, 14(3): 146–148.

Frankel, Paul H. 1966. *Mattei: Oil and Power Politics*. New York: Praeger.

Gobbi, Olimpia. 2011. "Emigrazione femminile: balie e domestiche marchigiane in Egitto fra Otto e Novecento," *Proposte e ricerche*, 24(66): 7–24.

Grange, Daniel. 1974. "Structure et techniques d'une propagande: Les émissions arabes de Radio-Bari," *Relations internationales*, 2: 165–185.

Hansen, Beth. 1985. "Wage Differentials in Italy and Egypt: The Incentive to Migrate before World War I," *Journal of European Economic History*, 14(2): 347–360.

Karanasou, Floresca. 1992. "Egyptianisation: The 1947 Company Law and the Foreign Communities in Egypt." Unpublished PhD diss.: St. Anthony's College, Oxford.

Khoury, Philip Shukry. 1987. *Syria and the French Mandate: The Politics of Arab Nationalism, 1920–1945*. Princeton: Princeton University Press.

Khuri-Makdisi, Ilham. 2010. *The Eastern Mediterranean and the Making of Global Radicalism, 1860–1914*. Berkeley, CA: University of California Press.

Lockman, Zachary. 1993. *Workers and Working Classes in the Middle East: Struggles, Histories, Historiographies*. New York: State University of New York Press.

Martelli, George. 1938. *Whose Sea? A Mediterranean Journey*. London: Chatto and Windus.

Marzano, Arturo. 2015. *Onde fasciste: La propaganda araba di Radio Bari (1934–43)*. Rome: Carocci.

Monroe, Elisabeth. 1938. *The Mediterranean in Politics*. Oxford, UK: Oxford University Press.

Onelli, Federica. 2013. *All'alba del Neoatlantismo: La politica egiziana dell'Italia (1951–1956)*. Milan: Angeli.

Owen, Roger. 1981. *The Middle East in the World Economy*. London: Methuen & Co. Ltd.

Petricioli, Marta. 2007. *Oltre il Mito: l'Egitto degli Italiani, 1917–1947*. Milan: B. Mondadori.

Pizzigallo, Matteo. 2008. *La diplomazia italiana e i paesi arabi dell'Oriente Mediterraneo (1946–1952)*. Milan: Angeli.

Richardson, J. E., and M. Colombo. 2013. "Continuity and Change in Anti-Immigrant Discourse in Italy: An Analysis of the Visual Propaganda of the Lega Nord," *Journal of Language and Politics*, 12(2): 180–202.

Santorelli, F. 1894. *L'Italia in Egitto: Impressioni e Note*. Cairo: Tip. Italiana.

Schewe, Eric Andrew. 2014. "State of Siege: The Development of the Security State in Egypt during the Second World War." Unpublished PhD diss.: University of Michigan.

Sciartuni, Said. 1937. "L'Italia e i suoi rapporti futuri con i paesi arabi," *La vita italiana*, March.

———. 1939. "Egitto e Italia nel Mare Mediterraneo," *La vita italiana*, 53 (January–June).

Viviani, Paola. 2014. "L'Egitto di naturalisti, patrioti e religiosi italiani: Figari Bey, Balboni e Monsignor Dalfi," *La rivista di Arablit*, 4(7–8): 117–133.

Votaw, Dow. 1964. *Six Legged Dog, Mattei and ENI: A Study in Power*. Berkeley, CA: University of California Press.

CHAPTER 3
# Kaleidoscopic Out-Migration: The Departure of Foreigners from Mid Twentieth Century Egypt

*Angelos Dalachanis*

On July 18, 1961, a few days before the nationalization laws in Egypt, which are considered by many scholars and people outside academia to be the main cause of the Greeks' definitive departure from Egypt, Vyron Theodoropoulos, the consul general of Greece in Alexandria, addressed a confidential report to his ambassador in Cairo:

> *Our Alexandrian community is in steep decline. This is not due to the antiforeigner, let alone anti-Greek, policy of the Egyptian government or to any Arabic or Muslim chauvinism. On the contrary, we have much tangible proof of the favorable treatment our community receives from government officials. At the same time, I see how harmonious the coexistence is at the popular level between our people and the Arabs, who honestly respect and appreciate us. However, what is pushing us out of Egypt is the unavoidable economic and social evolution of the country. We can neither suspend this evolution nor expect that Egyptians will slow it down for our sake.*[1]

This quotation is interesting in the context of the Greek community, the largest foreign community in Egypt during the nineteenth and mid twentieth centuries, because it indicates that what is commonly called the 'exodus' was well underway before the nationalization laws and

---

[1] Archives of the Greek Ministry of Foreign Affairs (AYE)/ Central service (CS)/1961/21/15/2/1, 725, Alexandria, July 18, 1961, Theodoropoulos to Cairo embassy. On the issue of Greeks' departure from Egypt, see Dalachanis 2017.

provides one more piece of evidence for the favorable way the Egyptian governments treated Greeks. It is also interesting in the broader context of foreign communities in Egypt, because it reveals that, contrary to well-established views, the overall picture of the departure of foreigners is more complicated. Thus, in order to deal with this matter, two interrelated questions need to be addressed: Who were the foreigners in mid twentieth century Egypt and why did they leave?

These questions may seem simple, but they are not easy to answer for several reasons. Firstly, the notion of 'foreigner' took on different and often blurred meanings, as Egypt passed from the status of an autonomous province under Ottoman and later British semi-colonial rule to an independent nation-state; secondly, those who left did so over a wide time span and the departure rate fluctuated, with peaks and troughs; thirdly, the human capital of this movement did not originate from a single city but rather from many Egyptian cities and villages; and finally, the migrants reached many different destinations worldwide and migration took many different forms: voluntary and/or forced, return and/or reverse,[2] internal and/or overseas. Although 'foreigner' is a fluid, plural, and complex—and therefore unsatisfactory—category, I have come to use it because it is found in most of the period's sources. Indeed, Egyptian censuses, demographic data, and other empirical evidence identify Egypt's 'foreigners' and show that, pull factors from various destinations notwithstanding, their out-migration was not only fueled by moments of crisis in Egypt; it was also the result of many slow and less spectacular political, legal, economic, and cultural changes associated with the Egyptian state formation. Therefore, I discuss the departure of foreigners as a result of structural changes and crisis moments that variously had short, medium, and long-term effects on decisions to leave the country. I argue that the different timings of departure, the dissimilar migration patterns, the various state, international, and local institutions involved in this departure, and the destinations of the emigrants illustrate the multifaceted identities of Egypt's foreigners. After placing Egypt's foreigners in their context, I shall present the demographic trends from the 1920s to 1960 and will show how radical or less radical changes affected departure. A closer look at this out-migration allows us

---

2   A reverse migration is a movement toward a country of origin where migrants have not lived or visited by the time they move to it. For a discussion on migration categories and theories, see Harzig and Hoerder 2009.

to challenge the one-dimensional view that depicts one person, Gamal Abdel Nasser, or the military regime he established as solely responsible for the definitive departure of foreigners from Egypt.

## Egypt and Its Foreigners

Through the nineteenth century and the first decades of the twentieth century, migrants of multiple ethnic, religious, and national origins, from regions around the Mediterranean and beyond, and of various economic and social backgrounds, ranging from rich hotshots, powerful merchants, and industrialists to unskilled workers and destitute people, moved to Egypt. Literature, public history, and a number of historical works encapsulate this social and urban reality, especially those that consider Alexandria from a 'cosmopolitan' perspective that gives a positive and glamorous image of foreign presence. Yet this perspective has also been strongly contested.[3] Furthermore, more nuanced categorizations of Egypt's population (including foreigners) at the turn of the twentieth century have recently been put forward (Hanley 2017). In this chapter, 'foreigners' are those who were classified in the post-1922 Egyptian censuses as such, which means people of different nationalities (British, French, Italians, most of the Greeks, etc.), but also those who were classified as Egyptian nationals but of different "race," as the 1927 census puts it, which include non-Egyptian ethnic or religious minorities such Armenians, Jews, Syrians and others.[4] The majority of foreign nationals were Greeks, followed by Italians (see table 1).[5]

Most of the foreign nationals were citizens of their respective countries, but in the Greek case an important proportion of them (11 percent) were included in the 1927 census as Egyptian nationals. Both communities covered a wide socioeconomic range, chiefly middle and low-income. Greeks and Italians, along with other non-Egyptian communities such as Jews,[6] Armenians (Le Gall-Kazazian 1992; 1995),

---

3  This use of this term has been challenged by Driessen 2005; Fahmy 2004; Hanley 2012.
4  *Annuaire statistique, 1927–1928* (1929); *Annuaire statistique, 1937–1938* (1939).
5  On the Greek community in Egypt, see Kitroeff 1989; Dalachanis 2017. On the Italian community in Egypt, see Petricioli 2007; Viscomi 2016.
6  On the Jewish community of Egypt, see Laskier 1992; Kramer 1989; Beinin 1998; Miccoli 2015.

## Table 1. Population of Egypt, 1927–1960

|  | 1927 | 1937 | 1947 | 1960 |
|---|---|---|---|---|
| Egyptians | 13,952,264 | 15,734,170 | 18,966,767 | 25,984,101 |
| European nationals: | | | | |
| Greeks | 76,264 | 68,559 | 57,427 | 47,673 |
| Italians | 52,462 | 47,706 | 27,958 | 14,089 |
| British/Maltese | 34,169 | 31,523 | 28,246 | 25,175 |
| French | 24,332 | 18,821 | 9,717 | |
| Others | — | — | 16,664 | |
| Non-Egyptian minorities: | | | | |
| Jews | 63,550 | 62,953 | 65,639 | 8,561 |
| Armenians | 17,145 | 16,886 | — | — |
| Syrians, Palestinians, and other Arab nationalities | 39,605 | 38,692 | — | 56,375 |

Sources: *Annuaire statistique*, 1929, 1939, 1951; *Qaraa 'ama li-l soukan* 1960; Karanasou 1992:11. The numbers refer to the sedentary population.

Syrians (Philipp 1985), and other Arabs, constitute the populations that the Egyptian historiography refers to as *mutamassirun*. *Mutamassirun* literary means the 'Egyptianized,' a term that qualifies those who "recognize[d] both an affinity and conformity with the Egyptian way of life and yet, at the same time, a certain detachment from it" (Gorman 2003:175). Despite their legal status and specific ethnic or religious affiliations, the *mutamassirun* held a fluid but distinctive position among foreign and Egyptian elites and the Egyptian masses. Sharing this socioeconomic profile were the Maltese and the Cypriots, who were British subjects, just like the Adenese, Indians, and Somalis. In the same category of imperial subjects were the Algerians and the Tunisians, who were French subjects.

On the basis of socioeconomic profile, a fundamental distinction can be drawn between the above-mentioned groups and the nationals of colonial powers and other Western countries, essentially the British of metropolitan origin[7] (military personnel, administrators, and executives) (Mak 2012), the French of metropolitan origin, the Belgians, and the Swiss, who were mostly bourgeois. The foreign elite, comprising members of almost all the groups mentioned here, dominated economic activity in Egypt and controlled to a large extent the local political system through the nineteenth and the early twentieth centuries.

The prominent place of the non-Egyptian elite in the country is mainly the result of the policies of Mehmet Ali and his successors, of the extremely favorable conditions created—especially in Egypt—by the Capitulations, and of the British colonial presence from 1882 onward. The Capitulations were bilateral agreements between the Ottoman Empire and separate countries, which regulated the status of nationals of these countries in the Ottoman territory and granted privileges to them.[8] However, contrary to the situation prevailing in the rest of the empire, the privileges granted in Egypt exceeded the letter and the spirit of the agreements. "The European, who is privileged in Turkey, is ultra-privileged in Egypt," Lord Cromer pointed out.[9] Under the Capitulations in Egypt, foreign nationals enjoyed freedom of mobility and commerce, personal and religious freedom, protection from arrest, inviolability of their homes and businesses, exemption from all taxes except those few approved by the capitulatory powers, and legislative and judicial immunity.[10]

The overall position of foreign nationals became even more privileged in comparison with the local population after the beginning of the British occupation in 1882, under the pretext of protecting foreign

---

7 Foreign Office documents in the 1950s refer to these British as "Anglo-Saxons" or "UK-based."

8 In 1536, France became the first country to sign such an agreement with Constantinople, and other countries followed its example in securing extraterritorial legal rights for their citizens. A total of fourteen different states—Austria, Belgium, Brazil, Denmark, France, Greece, Prussia (and later Germany), Italy, Netherlands, Portugal, Spain, Sweden, the United Kingdom, and the United States—negotiated capitulatory privileges for their citizens at different times.

9 Baring 1908:428. Evelyn Baring was a British diplomat and colonial administrator (1841–1917). He served as consul general in Egypt—but in fact as the head of the colonial-type administration—from 1882 to 1907.

10 For a summary of the Capitulations in Egypt, Persia, and the rest of the Ottoman Empire, see Wansbrough 1986.

minorities. Until the First World War, the British ruled Egypt as de facto colonial rulers, and in 1914 the country became a British protectorate. In February 1922, nominal independence was granted to the country, and from that point onward, even though it was gradually restrained, the British influence remained important until the early 1950s and came to a definitive end only after the 1956 Suez Crisis. Some foreign groups, namely the Greeks and the Italians, often claimed to have arrived in Egypt long before the British or the French in order to dissociate themselves from the colonial powers. However, in Egyptian eyes the foreign presence was associated with the British rule not only because of Britain's military intervention in 1882, but also because London placed foreign interests under its direct protection with a declaration issued after Egypt's nominal independence in 1922.

Thus the British colonial administration and the Capitulations created a privileged, semi-colonial type of political, economic, social, and cultural environment for their beneficiaries. It goes without saying that both undermined Egyptian national sovereignty after 1922, leading the national movement to tenaciously request the withdrawal of the British and the abolition of the Capitulations. The latter were abolished in 1937 but, because of an agreed twelve-year transitional period, they remained in force until 1949, when the Mixed Courts ceased operating,[11] thus outliving the Ottoman Empire by almost 30 years. In the meantime, Egypt had agreed in the Swiss city of Montreux, where the Capitulations were abolished, to sign treaties of establishment with each one of the capitulatory countries before the end of the transition period. These treaties were to create a new, lighter version of the Capitulations for foreign communities, and thus a new protection regime for foreign nationals. However, they never took shape because of the reaction of the Egyptian people through the press and demonstrations, and because they would regenerate in the popular imagination the "specter of the abhorred Capitulations

---

11 The Mixed Courts were founded in 1875 to deal with cases in which litigants were of different nationalities. They were conceived as national Egyptian courts that operated under conditions fixed by international agreements for the trial of 'mixed' cases. They constituted a hybrid institution, which administered their own law, *Les Codes Mixtes d'Egypte*, based on the French *Code Napoléon* derived from Roman law, while also drawing on sharia and Egyptian customary law. On the Mixed Courts in Egypt, see Naguib 2002.

regime," according to Adly Andraos, then the ambassador of Egypt in Athens.[12]

In a broader but still regional context, the immediate postwar years were also marked by the creation of the state of Israel in 1948. The reemergence of Egyptian national and social claims, especially after the defeat in the Palestine War, generated demonstrations, which were fueled by anti-British feelings and sometimes resulted in attacks on foreign properties. The end of the transitional period in 1949 and the abandonment of the treaties of establishment in practice signified that the legal position of foreign nationals ceased to be a bilateral issue and would thereafter largely depend on Egypt, which had to act as a sovereign state. As Hamid Sultan, professor of public international law at Cairo University at that time, pointed out: "Egypt must force its foreign inhabitants to respect its sovereignty, and it must subject them to its laws for a certain period of time. Not in order to take revenge, but simply in order to reaffirm its sovereignty and to enable the state to produce laws that are necessary for the regularization of its interests with those of foreigners, and the protection of Egyptian nationals and their interests" (Kader 1953:18). Egypt had decided to treat foreigners in its territory according to the standards of international law, in the same way as the former capitulatory countries.

The world of 1950 was very much different from that of 1937. The Second World War had considerably decreased colonial influence around the world and Egypt sought to follow with determination the road to national independence and the consolidation of the nation-state. In this context, a guerrilla struggle against the presence of the British and their repression of Egyptians in the Suez Canal Zone broke out in that area in 1951. It ended with the burning and looting of buildings and shops in downtown Cairo, the modern European center of the city, on the night of January 26, 1952—an incident that became known as "Black Saturday" (Kerboeuf 2005). As a result, 463 shops belonging to foreigners were destroyed, a fact that provoked acute unease among them. The long period of political stability since 1945 came to an end

---

12 Archives of the French Ministry of Foreign Affairs (MAE)/Levant 1944–1965/Egypte 1944–1952/Dossier 124/Rapport avec les pays étrangers/série k/carton 72/Dossiers 11 à 18/Egypte juin 1947/février 1953/Rapports avec la Grèce/124/Bulletin II, Adly Y. Andraos, Ambassador of Egypt to Athens, Athens, 16/6/1952.

with the Free Officers' military coup on July 23, 1952 and the abolition of the Egyptian monarchy. In the meantime, the colonial powers were gradually replaced by the superpowers, the Soviet Union and the US, and the new bipolar system of the Cold War dominated international affairs.

Gamal Abdel Nasser, who officially came to power in November 1954, aware of the opportunities provided by the new bipolar context and fading colonialism, presented himself as one of the main figures of the 'Third World' that was emerging from decolonization, and as an embodiment of Arab unity (Panarabism). In October 1954, the British, under Egyptian nationalist pressure, agreed to withdraw their military forces from Egypt by 1956. Nasser's personal diplomatic triumph in the Suez Crisis marked the end of the colonial presence in the Middle East and gave him the opportunity to present himself as the leader of the Arab world, a consequence of which was the creation of the United Arab Republic through the merger of Egypt and Syria in 1958. The post–Suez Crisis era was marked by a more pronounced state intervention in the Egyptian economy, the centerpieces of which were the Egyptianization measures of January 1957, the series of socialist laws beginning in 1959, and the nationalization laws of July 1961.

## Departure in the Censuses

The non-Egyptian population reached its peak in the late 1920s (see table 1), and until 1960, while the Egyptian population exploded (+86.2%), the number of foreign nationals and non-Egyptian communities gradually shrank by 50.6% due to the departure of their members. This numerical decrease did not affect all groups, and certainly not all of them in the same manner. For instance, while British, French, and Belgians almost completely disappeared from the map of Egypt's foreigners, nationals from Arab countries considerably increased their demographic power.

The Greek community lost more than a third (-37.4%) of its members between 1927 and 1960. Italian losses were almost double the Greek ones, reaching a decrease of 73% during the same period. As for the French and the British, the radical blow they suffered mostly concerned people of metropolitan origin, most of whom were obliged to leave the country during the Suez Crisis. Other non-Egyptian minorities, like the Jewish population, practically vanished during the same period: only 13.5% of the 1927 population remained in 1960. The vast majority had left Egypt for good, either willingly or by force. It is interesting to point out again that during the same period—and especially in the postwar years—the number of Arab nationals gradually increased enough to form important and rather influential communities by the early 1960s. Before discussing the different waves of departure, it is worth mentioning that in the census of 1960, the first to be published solely in Arabic, the only groups classified as European were the Greeks and Italians, while the Syrians, Palestinians, and Sudanese were the only ones classified as Arab. All the others were not mentioned as separate groups but were included in the broader category of "other nationalities." After a mass departure movement that followed a series of socialist laws in the early 1960s, the number of European nationals and non-Egyptian minorities diminished even further.

During the years of the censuses mentioned in the table, one can distinguish several departure waves of European nationals and non-Egyptian communities from Egypt, which do not correspond to clear-cut chronological phases or to single groups. There is, however, a common ground in a number of departure stories. Some of them were due to radical changes with immediate effects, such as the Second World War in the Italian case, the Palestine War in the case of Jews, and the Suez Crisis for the French, the British, and the Jews. Other departures, such as that of the Greeks, were more related to slow structural changes that were part of the Egyptian national project in economic, social, cultural, and legal terms. Changes such as legislation regarding foreign nationals, the mandatory use of literary Arabic in business communications, and state control over economic activities did not immediately influence the foreigners' decision to leave Egypt. The short, medium, and long-term reasons transcended the boundaries of these communities. For example, not all Jews left at a time of crisis, while a considerable number of Greeks left because of the Suez Crisis. As for the Italians, there was a high rate of repatriation among them between 1936 and 1939. The following analysis focuses on the dominant tendencies behind each group's departure and helps us paint a more nuanced picture of the real reasons behind the end of the foreigners' privileged presence in Egypt.

## Structural Change and Departure

The abolition of the Capitulations was a major structural change with medium and long-term effects on the departure of foreign nationals. For as long as the Capitulations were in force, they functioned as a protective cloak for foreigners in judicial and economic terms, as well as a cohesive element offering different communities the possibility of living as privileged minorities. Along with the British presence, the Capitulations had guaranteed the economic prosperity of the foreign economic elites and their control over the rest of their community's members. The domination of foreigners had not only economic and political but also cultural aspects. Most of them were educated either in community schools or in the Christian missionary and other foreign or local establishments, where the teaching languages were mainly French and English (Dalachanis 2017:120–147; Petricioli 1997; Trimi-Kyrou 1996; Turiano and Viscomi 2018). This bred a superiority complex over the Egyptian population, which was more evident in the reluctance of the majority of foreigners to learn literary Arabic properly. In this respect, they were unable to communicate with the Egyptian state after 1942 when it imposed the use of literary Arabic as a language of communication between the state administration and business. From 1958 onward, only Arabic was used in every economic or state activity. Indeed, even if many foreigners could use the Egyptian dialect in their daily life, only a small number of them could read or write in literary Arabic, let alone conduct business in it (Viscomi 2016:212; Dalachanis 2017:139–143). It was reasonable to expect that the gradual expansion of Arabic would marginalize those who had poor knowledge of it in social life and professional activities. Even foreign entrepreneurs preferred to hire Egyptians, because they had by then received a better education than in the previous decades, had the advantage of being native speakers, and also accepted lower wages than foreigners.

Despite the twelve-year transitional period granted at Montreux in order for the nationals of the former capitulatory countries to adjust to the requirements of the new era and to wean themselves off the Capitulations, few initiatives were undertaken in this direction. Because of the prospective of a treaty of establishment and the extraordinary conditions in the country during the Second World War, most of them hoped that a treaty would be enough to offer them a new protection regime. However, in the aftermath of the Second World War, and especially after the Arab defeat in the Palestine War, the Egyptian national movement moved fast in two directions: the abolition of the plan for the conclusion of treaties of establishment—which were considered a revival of the Capitulations—and a push for British withdrawal. Both were expressed almost simultaneously in 1951.

The military coup of the Free Officers in July 1952 brought about new political and economic conditions. The bonds of the foreign economic elite with the old regime were rendered meaningless and the new status quo required a rapprochement with a new military elite under the leadership of Muhammad Naguib, and shortly afterward of Gamal Abdel Nasser. Initially, the new regime promoted foreigners' investments, while Nasser became a leading figure of the anti-colonial struggle and gradually tried to keep a balance between the Western and Eastern blocs. In the new Egyptian context, foreigners often remained prisoners of the capitulatory past and their traditionally close relationship with Western countries, which was reaffirmed in the Cold War context. Within this new framework, the foreigners, instead of emancipating themselves and consolidating their position through a rapprochement with the Egyptians and long-term readjustment plans, tried to continue in the most familiar way: through the protection of an external element, a role that individual states now had to play directly. Nonetheless, in an era of strong Egyptian nationalism and the dynamic presence of Egypt on the international scene, it would be difficult for any other country to impose its will on it.

While the Egyptian population increased and better education and training opportunities made professions once dominated by foreigners accessible to them (Ryzova 2005), postwar Egyptian governments implemented laws in favor of their nationals. The first serious effort was the 1947 Egyptianization Law 138 concerning joint stock companies, which set quotas on the percentage of Egyptian and foreign employees, even before the end of the twelve-year transitional period for the full abolition of the Capitulations (Karanasou 1992:11). The main objective was to secure employment for the ever-increasing and better-educated Egyptian labor force, which could not be absorbed by either the public or the agricultural sector, but also to transfer control of the joint stock companies to Egyptian hands. The law gave joint stock companies three years to ensure that 51% of the capital, 40% of the boards of directors, 75% of the employees, and 90% of the workers would be Egyptian.[13]

Even if Law 138/1947 did not produce the anticipated results in the labor market, it discouraged European investments and increased anxiety among foreign citizens regarding the government's intentions toward their future in the country. Even though foreigners' stays in Egypt were regulated in terms of residence (five or ten years) after 1952–1953, the gradual Egyptianization of the labor market and the joint stock companies made Egyptian citizenship more and more necessary to those who wanted to remain in the country. More discriminatory laws promoting Egyptians in the labor market in order to deal with unemployment were promulgated in the 1950s and 1960s. Thus, Egyptian citizenship became the basic 'qualification' for obtaining a job, and the Egyptian state remained generally reluctant to grant this status to foreigners who asked for it. At the same time, only a relatively small number of middle- and lower-class foreigners requested it, as the new Egyptian citizens were obliged, among other things, to do military service.

Therefore, the ending of the Capitulations generated the implementation of measures that were part of the state formation process in terms of control over economic activities and contributed to the decision of foreigners to leave the country. According to Themistoklis Matsakis, a prominent figure in the Greek community in Cairo, such measures concerned, among others, increased control over exports and imports; the obligation to keep accounting records; the organization and the control of tax issues; increased control over foreign exchange; the laws regarding joint stock companies, schools, associations, and the like; the Egyptianization of banks, insurance companies, and foreign commercial representations that was implemented in 1957; and the exclusion of foreign citizens from certain professions (Matsakis 1965:5).

Despite the image of a so-called 'cosmopolitan' society, of openness to the 'other,' or of an interethnic ethos, which has often been invoked in discussions, especially about Alexandria in the late nineteenth and early twentieth centuries, the foreign communities were rather introverted, as the high rates of endogamy and their "parochial social life"

---

13 The law defined as an employee "someone who was doing an administrative or technical job, or working as a clerk or accountant, and was paid a salary, meaning a monthly income" (Karanasou 1992:101–102).

(Kazamias 2009:23) demonstrate. The shortage of available bachelors was the result of men emigrating for better career prospects, a solution highly favored by the pro-immigration policy of other countries, mainly Australia, which hosted a considerable number of European immigrants from Egypt. Finally, to better understand the emigration of foreigners, we should take into account that departures provoked additional departures. Ongoing migration precipitated by crisis situations that will be described in the following section completely altered the local social and economic reality in a way that made non-Egyptian communities feel more and more foreign.

## Leaving after Moments of Crisis

Slow changes in the economic and cultural context with medium and long-term effects alienated foreigners from their environment and were often coupled with sudden changes due to the local effects of international crises in which Egypt was directly or indirectly involved. Indeed, the fate of the non-Egyptian communities in Egypt was increasingly linked to evolutions in the diplomatic arena. National, ethnic, or religious groups that took advantage of the European powers' protection either as nationals and beneficiaries of the Capitulations, or as protégés of their home governments, found themselves heavily instrumentalized by their respective countries or by Egypt itself. The absence of a protection regime contributed to this situation. Another decisive factor was linked to the fact that until 1936 Egypt could not pursue an independent foreign policy without taking into account British interests. The Anglo-Egyptian treaty concluded that year provided Cairo for the first time with the opportunity to establish embassies abroad and develop its own foreign policy. Yet this opportunity had limits: the treaty stipulated that, if Egypt was considered to be in danger, Britain had the right to deploy its army on Egyptian territory to "protect" it, as would occur during the Second World War. Consequently, Britain's enemies were supposed to become enemies of Egypt as well. The obvious victim during this period was the Italian population.

The number of Italians decreased by 41% between the 1937 and 1947 censuses. During the war, a significant number of adult male members of the community were detained in concentration camps because they belonged to a state that was an enemy of Britain. In 1943, for instance, more than 7,000 Italians were detained in camps such as Fayed, a development that completely dismantled the demographic backbone of the community (Viscomi 2016:151). When released from the camps, they found that Egyptians and other foreign nationals had taken many of their jobs. Their situation was often harder than that of other foreigners, because a significant number of Italian stores and companies shut down for good during the war. Under normal circumstances, these businesses would have absorbed unemployed Italians who were released from the camps. Additionally, Italian banks, which could have provided these businesses with credit, also stopped operating in the country and did not resume their activities until 1948.[14] To these unfavorable conditions can be added competition with the Egyptians and other nationals, or the hostility of these nationals, especially the Greeks, in the aftermath of the war. The latter is a result of the invasion of Greece by fascist Italy in 1940 and the Italian occupation of Greek regions along with the German and Bulgarian occupation during the war. According to Viscomi, the difficult situation of the community was evident to contemporary observers, who claimed that 80% of the community was in a state of absolute "desperation" immediately after the war (Viscomi 2016:152). Many Italians abandoned the country, their community never managing to recover demographically. On the contrary, their number gradually shrank in the 1950s.

The Italians were not the only community to be affected by the war. The immediate postwar era was also marked by the departure of a significant number of low-income Maltese and Cypriots, who were mostly British subjects. Like the Italians, it was difficult for them to find a job after the war. Many of the Maltese and Greeks, who had served in the Allied military forces during wartime, remained unemployed after its end, because Egyptians or other foreigners had been recruited in their place and because of the economic downturn in the country (Dalachanis 2009:36–37; Karanasou 1992:345–354). These unemployed and sometimes almost destitute people often followed the migration routes to Australia and other destinations. This departure had a positive side effect, since it contributed to the easing of pressure on the labor market and opened new employment prospects

---

14 AYE/CS/1944/40/4, Alexandria, 26/10/1943, Maxouris to Tsouderos; Viscomi 2016:196.

for those remaining. When, for example, following Stalin's call, 1,700 Armenians left Alexandria for the Soviet Union on the night of September 3, 1947, on board the Soviet ship *Pabeda*, the Greek Chamber of Commerce dignitaries saw this as a major opportunity for the Greeks, who could fill in the spaces left by the departees ("Greek Inactive Capital" 1948:3).

Between the Palestine War of 1948 and 1954, 15,872 Egyptian Jews—amounting to roughly 20 to 25 percent of the total Jewish population of the country—left Egypt, mainly for the newborn state of Israel (Kramer 1989:218–219). Even before Jews started leaving the country, a Greek diplomat dealing with the high unemployment within the Greek community stated: "There is a great possibility that the [Greek] community will manage to survive in the end and maybe the antipathy that, according to my information, has started to be shown by the Egyptian governmental and financial circles against our biggest rival, the Jews, will help this survival."[15] With the 1956 Crisis, and in late 1956 and 1957, 40,000 to 50,000 Jews departed "either of their own accord or by force" (Kramer 1989:221). Along with the Jews, a significant number of "enemy subjects," namely British and French, were also expelled from Egypt at the same time.

As for the French, of the 9,000 French citizens in Egypt (including those in the Suez Canal Zone) just before the Crisis, approximately 8,000—77.7% of the French community in Egypt—fled to France between August 1956 and March 1957. The first 2,500 left before the military intervention of October/November 1956 and another 5,500 between November and March, when Egypt retaliated after Israel, Britain, and France invaded the country (Dubois 1992:131, 137; 1995:86; Jordi 1993:21–23). A particularity of the French community was the high number of women, many of whom were nuns engaged in education and health care. Considered as enemy subjects, many of the French people lost much of their property.

As for the British, in March 1956, shortly before the Suez Crisis, their population in Egypt was estimated as follows: 15,340 people, of whom 5,185 were Cypriots and 250 were Adenese, Somalis, and Indians who lived in Port Said or Suez and mostly worked for the Suez

---

15 AYE/CS/1948/94/4/4/2, 230, Alexandria, 11/10/1947, Zamarias to Triantafyllidis.

Canal company.[16] The expulsion because of the Suez Crisis basically concerned the category of "UK-based/Anglo-Saxons." Evacuation plans for British subjects at the time of the Suez Crisis covered not only Egypt but almost all countries of the Middle East (Iraq, Libya, Sudan, Gulf countries, Lebanon, Syria, and Jordan). Until the beginning of the military operations, the Foreign Office was not preparing for the evacuation of British subjects such as the Maltese or the Cypriots. As it was pointed out: "The Maltese and other (mainly Cypriot) British nationals are in less danger of reprisals than the Anglo-Saxons."[17] The report continued:

> *It is highly probable ... that the great majority of the Maltese and Cypriots would serve their own best interests if they stayed put and lay low. Both communities are closely assimilated to the local population and neither is likely to attract mob violence. The Cypriots are unlikely to attract hostile official attention in view of Egyptian attitude on* Enosis *question. The Maltese may at the worst suffer petty victimization and short internment.*[18]

After the sequestration measures of November 1956, the Egyptians treated Cypriots "as Greek citizens in possession of British passports."[19] However, most of the Maltese were asked to leave Egypt.

A few years later, in early 1961, Belgian assets in Egypt were sequestered and Belgian citizens were deported from the country as a result of the critical situation in the Belgian Congo.[20] The fate of Egypt

---

16 The National Archives of the UK (TNA)/Foreign Office (FO) 369-5246, 1956/K 2014/8/G, "British Subjects Registered at Consulates in Certain Middle East Countries," March 1956.
17 TNA/FO 369-5248, 1956/K 204/189/G. Secret. Report. Evacuation of British subjects from Egypt, J. H. A. Watson, 13/8/1956.
18 TNA/FO 369-5248, 1956/K 204/198/G. Secret. Telegram No 2608 from Foreign office to Cairo, 30/8/1956.
19 TNA/FO 369-5248, 1956/K 204/294/G. Secret. Telegram No 2389 from the Secretary of State for the Colonies, 30/11/1956.
20 Salmon 1995:194–195. In June 1960, Congo declared its independence. A month later, the Force Publique, the Congolese liberation army, forced 44,484 European citizens to leave the country between July 9 and 28, 1960. Belgian efforts to regain control of the country and the protests that took place in Léopoldville (now Kinshasa) provoked the breaking of diplomatic relations between Congo and the UAR on December 1, 1960.

was linked to the decolonization movement throughout the 1950s and especially after the Bandung conference in April 1955. Nasser assisted the liberation movements materially and morally in all the countries where colonial rule had been imposed. Because of Belgian policies in the Belgian Congo, Nasser nationalized the Belgian National Bank, the Egyptian Electric Company, and the Cairo Tramway Company on December 1, 1960, all companies with Belgian majority participation. In the following months, in reprisal for the assassination of Patrice Lumumba, Congo's independence leader and prime minister, the Egyptian leader sequestered 49 Belgian companies, and on February 27, 1961 the properties of 407 Belgian residents in Egypt.[21] They were banned from engaging in commercial and financial activities and almost all of them were asked to leave the country within 24 hours.

The mass exodus of Greeks and other foreigners in the early 1960s may be considered as the last wave. This movement was triggered by a combination of slow, long-term changes and rapid radical change. When state intervention in the economy became more pronounced, with an unprecedented number of consecutive laws from 1959 onward, the exodus of the remaining Europeans, namely the Greeks and the Italians, accelerated even more. Even though a relatively small number of people were directly affected by the new legislation, this departure movement was fed by increasing uncertainty about the future, motivated by numerous socialist laws passed after a long period of instability. Not many foreigners identified themselves with the socialist vision of Nasser. The decision of most of them to leave en masse was influenced by the general situation and by the personal circumstances and character of each individual. However, there was also a collective stimulus: the increasing anxiety about impending measures, which in the event never materialized to the anticipated extent. The rumors about what might happen in the future contributed to a state of near panic. As the economic and cultural context changed for all the reasons mentioned, people organized their departure.

---

21 Ducruet 1964:323–324. Nasser first considered nationalizing Belgian holdings in 1957, when their value was estimated at LE 17 million. On December 1, 1960, Belgian-held capital was valued at LE 8 million.

## Concluding Remarks

This chapter has briefly examined the principal push factors that triggered the departure of foreigners from Egypt in the mid twentieth century by focusing on the outcome of slow structural changes as well as moments of crisis. People usually migrate for a better future. When foreigners left Egypt, except those who were forced to leave, they did so because they were more or less convinced that there was no future for them in Egypt or there was a better future for them elsewhere. Due to the protracted but drastic state formation process, the world of privileges and protection enjoyed by foreigners gradually fell apart. These radical changes show disparities in terms of speed. Overall, it was a slow process that nonetheless took the form of rapid change during wartime, international conflicts such as the Arab–Israeli confrontation, and the crises related to decolonization. At the more critical moments, the communities that proved to be more fragile were those whose respective home countries were directly or indirectly engaged in conflict with Egypt. It is difficult to form a typology for the departure of all foreigners. Apart from political reasons, economic, cultural, and personal factors also contributed to their decision to leave the country.

Several destinations were open to migrants when these foreigners were about to leave. Countries such as Australia, Canada, the US, Argentina, and Brazil, some of which actively sought out immigrants in the postwar years, attracted a great number of Egypt's foreigners, making their decision to leave easier. Some decided to move to their promised homelands, namely Israel and Soviet Armenia, while many others, like the Greeks and the Italians, "returned" to an imagined homeland, since they had not lived or been born there. Others, like the French, British, and Belgians, returned to their home countries, joining other co-nationals who were also moving back in the aftermath of the decolonization movement and the resulting creation of independent states.

## References

*Annuaire statistique, 1927–1928*. 1929. Cairo: Imprimerie nationale.
*Annuaire statistique, 1937–1938*. 1939. Cairo: Imprimerie nationale.
*Annuaire statistique, 1947–1948*. 1951. Cairo: Imprimerie nationale.
Baring, E., Earl of Cromer. 1908. *Modern Egypt*. Vol. 2. London: Macmillan (reprinted in 2001 by Routledge).

Beinin, Joel. 1998. *The Dispersion of Egyptian Jewry*. Berkeley: University of California Press.

Dalachanis, Angelos. 2009. "The Emigration of Greeks from Egypt during the Early Post War Years." *Journal of the Hellenic Diaspora*, 35(2): 35–44.

———. 2017. *The Greek Exodus from Egypt: Diaspora Politics and Emigration*. New York and Oxford: Berghahn.

Driessen, Henk. 2005. "Mediterranean Port Cities: Cosmopolitanism Reconsidered," *History and Anthropology*, 16(1): 129–141.

Dubois, Colette. 1992. "Avant-Première: Suez, un cas de migration forcée (1956–1957)," *Civilization*, 40(2): 128–153.

———. 1995. "La nation et les Français d'Outre-Mer: Rapatriés ou sinistrés de la décolonisation?" In J.-L. Miège and C. Dubois, eds. *L'Europe retrouvée: Les migrations de la décolonisation*, 75–115. Paris: L'Harmattan.

Ducruet, Jean. 1964. *Les Capitaux européens au Proche-Orient*. Paris: Presses Universitaires de France.

Fahmy, Khaled. 2004. "Towards a Social History of Modern Alexandria." In A. Hirst and M. Silk, eds. *Alexandria, Real and Imagined*, 281–306. Cairo: American University in Cairo Press.

Gorman, Anthony. 2003. *Historians, State and Politics in Twentieth Century Egypt*. London: Routledge.

"The Greek Inactive Capital." 1948. *Bulletin of the GCCA*, 584, 31 August: 1–4.

Hanley, Will. 2012. "Cosmopolitan Cursing in Late Nineteenth Century Alexandria." In D. MacLean and S. Karmali Ahmed, eds. *Cosmopolitanism in Muslim Contexts: Perspectives from the Past*, 92–104. Edinburgh: Edinburgh University Press.

———. 2017. *Identifying with Nationality: Europeans, Ottomans and Egyptians in Alexandria*. New York: Columbia University Press.

Harzig, Christiane, and Dirk Hoerder. 2009. *What Is Migration History?* Cambridge and Malden: Polity Press (reprint 2012).

Jordi, Jean Jacques. 1993. *De l'exode à l'exil: Rapatriés et Pieds-Noirs en France*. Paris: L'Harmattan.

Kader, Yehia Abdel. 1953. *Les Passeports et la résidence des étrangers en Égypte*. Alexandria: Journal du commerce et de la marine.

Karanasou, Floresca. 1992. "Egyptianisation: The 1947 Company Law and the Foreign Communities in Egypt." Unpublished PhD dissertation: Oxford University.

Kazamias, Alexander. 2009. "The 'Purge of the Greeks' from Nasserite Egypt: Myths and Realities," *Journal of the Hellenic Diaspora*, 35(2): 13–34.

Kerboeuf, Anne-Claire. 2005. "The Cairo Fire of 26 January 1952 and the Interpretations of History." In A. Goldschmidt, A. J. Johnson, and B. I. Salmoni, eds. *Re-Envisioning Egypt, 1919–1956*, 194–216. Cairo: American University in Cairo Press.

Kitroeff, Alexander. 1989. *The Greeks in Egypt: Ethnicity and Class, 1917–1937*. Oxford: Ithaca Press.

Kramer, Gudrun. 1989. *The Jews in Modern Egypt, 1914–1952*. London: I.B. Tauris.

Laskier, Michael. 1992. *The Jews of Egypt, 1920–1970*. New York: New York University Press.

Le Gall-Kazazian, Anne. 1992. "Être arménien." In R. Ilbert and I. Yiannakakis, eds. *Alexandrie 1860–1960: Un modèle éphémère de convivialité: communautés et identité cosmopolite*, 68–80. Paris: Autrement.

———. 1995. "Les Arméniens d'Égypte (XIXe–XXe): La réforme à l'échelle communautaire." In A. Roussillon, ed. *Entre réforme sociale et mouvement national: Identité et modernisation en Égypte, 1882–1962*, 501–517. Cairo: CEDEJ.

Mak, Lanver. 2012. *The British in Egypt: Community, Crime and Crises, 1882–1922*. London and New York: I.B. Tauris.

Matsakis, Themistoklis. 1965. *To dilemma tou aigyptiotou ellinismou* [The Dilemma of Egyptian Hellenism]. Cairo.

Miccoli, Dario. 2015. *Histories of the Jews of Egypt: An Imagined Bourgeoisie, 1880s–1950s*. London: Routledge.

Naguib, Saphinaz-Amal. 2002. "Legal Pluralism in the Mediterranean: The Case of the Mixed Courts of Egypt: 1875–1949." In S. A. Naguib, ed. *The Intangible Heritage of the Mediterranean*, 169–180. Oslo: Unipub.

Petricioli, Marta. 1997. "Italian Schools in Egypt," *British Journal of Middle Eastern Studies*, 24(2): 179–191.

———. 2007. *Oltre il mito: L'Egitto degli Italiani, 1917–1947*. Milan: Bruno Mondadori.

Philipp, Thomas. 1985. *The Syrians in Egypt, 1725–1975*. Stuttgart: Steiner.

*Qaraa 'ama li-l soukan* [General Population Census of Egypt: General Tables]. 1960. Cairo: Government Press.

Ryzova, Lucie. 2005. "Egyptianizing Modernity through the 'New Effendiya': Social and Cultural Construction of the Middle Class in Egypt under the Monarchy." In A. Goldschmidt et al., eds. *Re-Envisioning Egypt: 1919–1952*, 124–163. Cairo: American University in Cairo Press.

Salmon, Pierre. 1995. "Les retours en Belgique induits par la décolonisation." In J.-L. Miège and C. Dubois, eds. *L'Europe retrouvée: Les migrations de la décolonisation*, 191–212. Paris: L'Harmattan.

Trimi-Kyrou, Katerina. 1996. "'Kinotis' Grecque d'Alexandrie. Sa politique educative (1843–1932)." Unpublished Ph.D. dissertation: Université des Sciences Humaines de Strasbourg (Strasbourg II).

Turiano, Annalaura, and Joseph John Viscomi. 2018. "Salesian Education and the Failed Integration of Italians in Egypt, 1937–1960," *Modern Italy* 23(1): 1–17.

Viscomi, Joseph John. 2016. "Out of Time: History, Presence, and the Departure of the Italians of Egypt, 1933–Present." Unpublished Ph.D. dissertation: University of Michigan.

Wansbrough, John. E. 1986. "Imtiyazat." In H. A. R. Gibb, ed. *The Encyclopedia of Islam*, 1178–1195. Leiden: Brill.

## CHAPTER 4

# Waiting in Izmir: Syrians in the Aegean Region after the "EU-Turkey Deal"

*Gerda Heck*

Migration is generally associated with mobility, people crossing borders, traveling several thousand miles, passing through cities, countries, and continents. In contrast, the reality of many migrants and refugees shows a very different picture. Their lives are often shaped by waiting: waiting for the smuggler, for money to make the journey, for a residence permit, for a positive (or a negative) decision regarding their asylum application, or for deportation. The arbitrariness and precarity of waiting is depicted in Samuel Beckett's play *Waiting for Godot* (1947/48), in which two characters, Vladimir and Estragon, endlessly wait the arrival of someone who will never come, wait for something to happen that will never happen. According to recent interpretations, the two might have been Jewish friends of Beckett, expecting a smuggler—some Godot—to bring them out of German-occupied France. Godot does not show up. Perhaps he will come tomorrow? Maybe not.

In recent decades, waiting and insecurity have emerged as key features of the border experiences suffered by many migrants from the global South (Andersson 2014). Mobility and migration have become a major global concern, especially in the hegemonic states of the global North. The European Union, the US, Australia, and also countries like South Africa have established "mobility regimes" by dramatically restricting their migration policies, with far-reaching consequences (Balibar 2003; Heck 2011; Hess and Kasparek 2010). The interactions between mobility, restriction, and containment produce a new form of biopolitics that puts migrants in a special situation characterized by a form of social hierarchy, which Etienne Balibar (2003:93), at the beginning of the 2000s, was already calling the "new system of Apartheid." For the migrants themselves, waiting for long times, sometimes years, in precarious situations, whether in transit or in their so-called destination country, often produces feelings of "powerlessness and vulnerability."

However, waiting does not necessarily mean passivity (Khosravi 2014). In recent research, which I conducted in the spring and summer of 2016 with my colleagues Firat Genc and Sabine Hess in Turkey, I observed the ways in which migrants try to make use of forced pauses. The multi-sited ethnography was conducted within the scope of the international research project "Transit Migration 2: A Research Project on the De- and Re-Stabilizations of the European Border Regime" (http://transitmigration-2.org). Our main research objective was to understand how the EU–Turkey Deal has impacted public policies, discourses, practices, and the daily reality of migrants. The research took place just after the deal came into effect, while an intense public debate was taking place in Turkey. But the research also addresses the content and possible effects of the agreement on the level of the European institutions, as well as locally among migrants. The focal point of the public debate in Turkey was the immediate effect of the deal: whether it would stop the border crossings. One of our main research locations was the Turkish coastal town Izmir. What we observed here was a deceleration of the migrant movement and a ubiquitous sense of stagnation, combined with unpredictability and uncertainty about the migrants' prospects. But that did not mean that people stopped hoping that their journey would continue. Moreover, while waiting to continue their passage, migrants in Izmir started to take root in their transit locality, although often on a very provisional basis.

Whereas most of the border literature and research focuses on state regulations of migration, thereby excluding the agency of the migrants themselves, the "ethnographic border regime analysis" approach, on which we draw for our research, stresses the impact of the migration movement itself on the border regime (Kasparek and Hess 2014; Tsianos & Hess 2010). Accordingly, the "border regime" becomes a "more or less ordered ensemble of practices and knowledge-power-complexes" resulting in a space of contestation, conflicts, and negotiations, whereas the movement of migration is one of its driving forces (Karakayali and

Tsianos 2007:3; Casas-Cortes et al. 2015:15). The city is an important field where these negotiations and contestations occur. The urban space can be read as constant, reflexive negotiation processes between the city and its inhabitants, both the old and the new (Simone 2002). Though it is not easy for migrants and refugees to find their way as newcomers, since their legal status is often uncertain, and they face constraints on access to accommodation, work, or education, cities are important arenas in which migrants negotiate and struggle for rights and recognition. Recent debates in urban and migration studies have broadened the understanding of the prevalent concept of citizenship (see Holston 2007; Isin 2008; Rygiel 2010). These new approaches emerged out of a critique of static and state-centered interpretations of citizenship and define it instead as a practice and a process. Thus, social movements, migrant self-organizations, and urban appropriation practices "from below" come increasingly into view (Hess and Lebuhn 2014). Social, political, and economic spaces in cities are produced and reproduced by people's everyday practices, interactions, and imaginations, be they long-time residents or newcomers. Moreover, the urban space is permanently altered through a constant fluctuation of people, goods, money, ideas, practices, and negotiations, which has an influence on both mobile and non-mobile inhabitants (Levitt and Glick-Schiller 2004; Pries 2010). It is also constructed and influenced by the trajectories, networks, and practices of migrants and other actors, who interact and communicate across different regional and national spaces.

In this chapter, I take a closer look at the (im)mobilities of Syrian refugees who seem to be trapped in Basmane, an inner-city district of Izmir, but still hold on to the idea of moving on. At the same time, they establish themselves locally.[1] They locally participate in the production of urban space, trying to appropriate rights and enact "urban citizenship."

## Basmane

Izmir, located on the Turkish Aegean coast close to several Greek islands, has been for many years a transit hub for migrants who are willing to travel toward Europe. Here, migrants usually meet in Basmane, an inner-city neighborhood, nowadays populated by many Syrian shops

---

1   I would like to thank our friend Maher Kharbet, who introduced us to many Syrians, made translations, and supported us during our research.

and restaurants, internet cafés, and cheap hotels. Arabic graffiti is sprayed on some walls in the neighborhood. The cafés in the area are known for hosting a well-established network of facilitators and smugglers whom migrants need for their passage to Greece. A large proportion of transiting migrants spend only a few days, sometimes even a few hours, in the city before they head for different spots on the coast, such as Dikili, Bodrum, or Çeşme, from which they set sail toward the islands. During the summer of 2015, the number of transiting migrants increased tremendously. About 850,000 people, half of whom were Syrians, made the crossing (IOM 2016:5). Almost every day hundreds of migrants arrived in the city and, due to the lack of accessible hotel rooms, many started to camp in the streets circling Basmane Square. This movement slowed down after the so-called EU–Turkey Deal took effect in April 2016. However, it has never completely stopped.

In Basmane, I met Maya, a Syrian refugee, and her 16-year old son Ashraf, several times in spring and summer 2016. On January 6, 2016, Maya arrived with her three children in the Turkish town of Tasucu (Mersin), coming off a ferry from the Lebanese port of Tripoli. "We were lucky, we arrived two days before Turkey introduced visa requirements for Syrians," Maya said in the interview. "We fled from the violence of the Syrian war, but also from my husband, who had been collaborating with the Assad regime, while I was working secretly for the opposition."

Aiming to cross the sea toward Greece, they failed twice. In their first attempt they were intercepted by the Turkish coast guard. During their second attempt, the Greek coast guard pushed them (illegally) back into Turkish waters, where they were again intercepted by the Turkish coast guard and brought back to the mainland. The family had paid US $2,000 for the passage. After the second failure, the smugglers paid them half of the money back, keeping $1,000 as commission, in case they wanted to give it another try. Then, in March 2016, the "EU–Turkey Deal"—more accurately, the "EU–Turkey statement"—was implemented (European Council 2016). At a time when the number of crossings dramatically decreased, Maya was not sure any more what to do: risking the perilous boat trip again, just to get stuck on a Greek island not knowing what would happen to them, did not make sense at all. Therefore, she was waiting, hoping that the conditions would change again. "Here in Basmane, for me personally, it is not so bad. But for the children, I do not really see any prospect for their education here. The two younger ones go to school at the moment. Ashraf should also go to school, but here there is no option for him, and additionally, he has to work to support our living here," she explained. Like Maya, many of our interview partners waited, hoping that the deal would fail and crossings would increase again, while at the same time they searched for work, sent the children to a local school, and started to engage in the community in Basmane.

## The EU–Turkey Statement

In response to the tremendous number of migrants crossing the Aegean Sea toward Greece in the summer of 2015, the European governments promptly turned their attention to the implementation of new measures to regain control over the migration movement. At an extraordinary summit in November 2015 in Brussels, the EU and Turkey introduced an action plan in order to control the common borders and to improve the situation for Syrian refugees in the country. As a result, on January 8, 2016 Turkey reintroduced visa restrictions for Syrians entering Turkey over air or sea borders, aiming to curb the number of arrivals to Turkey. Finally, during a summit in March 2016, the EU states and Turkey reached a comprehensive agreement, the so-called "EU–Turkey Deal." The agreement allows, first of all, the deportation back to Turkey of every migrant who arrived on the Greek islands after March 20, 2016, in fast-track asylum procedure, unless she or he can prove that Turkey is not a safe third country for her or him. The fast-track procedure is based on the question of whether Turkey is a "safe third country" or "first country of asylum" for the applicants. This procedure rests upon Article 60(4) of the newly introduced Greek Asylum Law (L 4375/2016), which allows the ministries of Interior and National Defense to implement exceptional measures in cases of large numbers of arrivals filing asylum applications at the border. Only vulnerable applicants (e.g., disabled persons, persons with chronic diseases, single mothers with children) are exempt from this procedure (and the subsequent deportations), as they can continue to claim asylum under the regular asylum procedure (AIRE Center and ECRE 2016:10).

In return, the EU promised to accept up to 72,000 Syrians from Turkey in a so-called 1:1 procedure—namely, for every Syrian deported from the Greek islands, the EU would take in one Syrian from the

Turkish camps (Peers and Roman 2016). Furthermore, Turkey would enhance its border control and commit to improving the living conditions for Syrians within the country in order to make crossing into Greece a much less desirable option. In response, the EU promised Turkey to increase its financial support to €6 billion, to be spent on improving the physical infrastructure and the institutional capacity of the Turkish state institutions. In addition to the lucrative monetary incentives, the political discourse employed by the Turkish government in order to justify the agreement to the public was based on the prospect of a visa liberalization for Turkish citizens for the Schengen area and an acceleration of the EU accession negotiations.

The deal itself is based on an older readmission agreement between Greece and Turkey. While it has been widely criticized by many human rights organizations, NGOs, and migration experts for its assumption that Turkey is a safe third country for refugees (Amnesty International 2017; Heck and Hess 2016; Mülteci-Der and Pro Asyl 2016; Peers and Roman 2016; Ulusoy 2016), a 2017 ruling by the Court of Justice of the European Union (CJEU), on the basis for annulment brought by three asylum seekers who were affected by the deal, declared that the EU–Turkey statement was not in fact an EU act. Hence the court had no jurisdiction to rule on the lawfulness of the agreement (CJEU 2017).

Despite the overblown expectations projected onto the deal in the spring of 2016, it has proven to be ineffective right from the beginning, especially from the point of view of migration management. In 390 out of 393 decisions in 2016, the Greek Asylum Appeals committees stopped the deportation of asylum seekers back to Turkey, stating that the country does not fulfill the requirements to be considered a safe third country (Gkliati 2017).

By the end of April 2017, only 5,035 Syrian refugees had been resettled from Turkey to the EU, since many EU countries refuse to admit them. During the same period, only 1,094 migrants who had arrived on the Greek islands via Turkey had been returned under the terms of the EU–Turkey statement (DRC 2017). But the deal has indeed reduced the number of crossings considerably, although they have been on the rise again since the coup d'état attempt in Turkey on July 15, 2016. In addition, and as an effect of the deal and the implementation of the EU "hotspot approach" laid down in the European Agenda of

Migration (Antonakaki, Kasparek, and Maniatis 2016; Tazzioli 2016), arriving migrants are largely locked in under very poor living conditions on the Greek islands (Heck and Hess 2016). Hence, one major effect of the deal has been the deceleration of movement on both sides of the Aegean Sea, on the Greek islands and in Turkey, and with it the prolongation of the waiting period for many migrants there.

## Trapped in Limbo? Daily Life in Basmane

Nowadays, a considerable number of Syrians live for longer periods in Izmir. Long before the onset of the civil war in Syria, a small Syrian community had already been established in the city.[2] According to the Association for Solidarity with Asylum Seekers and Migrants (ASAM), 98,000 Syrian refugees were officially registered in Izmir by May 2016. But ASAM assumed that more than 150,000 actually reside in the city.[3] Although they are scattered around the city, a large proportion of them live in the Basmane district (Yıldız and Uzgören 2016). Like Maya, many of them had come directly from Syria, while others had made a stopover in other cities of Turkey, and had lived before in a refugee camp in Lebanon or in Egypt. Many of them had already made several efforts to cross to the Greek islands. They had been stopped by the Turkish border patrol, cheated by smugglers, or foundered while still in Turkish waters and then been rescued by the Turkish coast guard. Some of our interview partners told us about family members of other boat passengers, who had drowned during the passage. Thus, trauma, grieving, hope, and desire, but also realism and eagerness to succeed and find a better life, are all closely entangled in everyday life in Basmane.

Many of our conversation partners expressed a sense of being trapped in limbo. One of them is Omran, who had to flee Syria due to his political activism against the Assad regime. Omran's wife Vera and their two children left Syria in November 2015 without him, since he was sought by the authorities, and did not know whether he would manage to escape the country alive. They left Damascus by bus for Beirut, then took an airplane to Istanbul. As soon as they arrived in Turkey, they hired a smuggler to make the perilous sea crossing to the Greek islands and further

---

2   Interview with Muhammed Ali Salih, Association for Solidarity with Syrians, Izmir, May 2, 2016.
3   Interview with ASAM, Izmir, May 3, 2016.

on to Germany. For the whole journey from Turkey to Germany, they paid $1,700. Even though the trip was extremely difficult and exhausting, they managed to arrive in Germany within 12 days.

When Omran attempted to cross the Turkish–Syrian border in the spring of 2016, it was much more difficult and expensive. Due to the fact that he was wanted by the Assad regime, and that, since January 8, 2016, Syrian nationals had had to apply for a visa to enter Turkey, he had to leave the country overland. Furthermore, from the last months of 2015, the open-gate policy on the Turkish land border—which had been introduced at the start of the Syrian war by the AKP government, citing humanitarian and religious discourses—was canceled, and it was almost impossible to cross legally. That led Omran to pay about $1,600 just to be smuggled across the Syrian–Turkish border. Shortly after his arrival in Izmir, the EU–Turkey Deal came into force and Omran felt stuck. He had already spent his last penny to get to Izmir, but more importantly, as for Maya, it did not seem to make sense for him to cross the Aegean Sea just to get stuck once again, this time on a Greek island, not knowing where and how his journey would end. Although his wife and daughters resided in Germany as asylum seekers, he would not be eligible for family reunification, since, as an employee of the German embassy in Ankara explained to him, he did not possess a Syrian passport any more. Having been imprisoned several times for being an anti-regime journalist, he would never get a passport from the Syrian government. Therefore he concluded: "Either I manage to go to Germany clandestinely or I have to remain here without my family." The story of Omran and Maya can be seen as representative in some ways for many other Syrians in Izmir, who are waiting for a chance to continue their journey. Besides Omran's primary aim, to reunite with his family, and Maya's wish for her children to get a better education, there also exist other reasons and motivations that make them want to continue.

## Legal Precarity—Syrian Refugees in Turkey

The 2013 Law on Foreigners and International Protection is a comprehensive legal change, which was originally stimulated by Turkey's EU accession process. It introduced two forms of international protection for non-Europeans, both meant to be temporary: conditional refugee status in the case of persons who are under direct threat, and subsidiary protection status in the case of persons coming to Turkey from countries where a general situation of violence prevails. However, Syrian refugees are excluded from these categories, since they are granted temporary protection status (TPS). Although, according to the TPS, Syrian migrants are entitled to access to basic health care services, education, and work permits, the actual living conditions in Turkey are difficult for them. Many of our interview partners told us that the temporariness of their legal status, which causes persistent insecurity and clouds their future prospects in Turkey, is the main reason for Syrians to leave the country. The temporary protection system precludes Syrians from a long-term perspective in Turkey, because the time a person spends in Turkey under the TPS does not count toward the requirements for a long-term residence permit. Furthermore, it prevents Syrians from applying for "international protection," since the UNHCR and Turkey agreed that persons under "temporary protection" would be neither registered by the UNHCR nor processed for refugee-status determination under its mandate. Only persons classified as "vulnerable," in accordance with the criteria defined by the UNHCR (i.e., disabled persons, persons with chronic diseases, single mothers, and persons whose lives and security are under direct threat in Turkey) are resettled in third countries. In the case of Omran, this means that, although he is a political refugee par excellence, he can apply neither for "international protection" nor for "resettlement," since he does not meet any of the UNHCR's "vulnerability" requirements. Nor can his family join him in Turkey, since they would be coming from a "safe third country" (i.e., Germany).

## Arriving without Wanting to Stay

Working conditions for Syrians are in general precarious and bad (Baban, Ilcan, and Rygiel 2016). Many Syrians work in Izmir's shoe and garment industry, in which wages are extremely low. The monthly wage is between 900 and 1,600 Turkish liras, for a six-day working week and shifts of 11 to 14 hours.[4] Although Syrian refugees are entitled to get work permits, the staff of the Izmir ASAM office told us in May 2016 that they have never come across anyone who had such a permit.[5] Working conditions seem to be worse for female refugees. Maya, for

---
4  Interview with Omran Alkasser (pseudonym), Izmir, May 10, 2016 and July 10, 2016.
5  Interview with ASAM, Izmir, May 3, 2016.

instance, tried to work twice in small knitting workshops. Both times she suffered sexual harassment from her employer. So she left her jobs, and instead her son Ashraf has become the breadwinner for the family of four. He is working 10 hours a day, six days a week in a Syrian restaurant, earning 35 Turkish liras per day.

Although Syrian children are officially entitled to attend school, many of them, like Ashraf, do not, since they have to work in order to feed their families. Nevertheless, while waiting, the refugees have started to establish themselves step by step. They have sought and found mostly low-paid work, either in the local shoe and garment industry or in restaurants. Some of them are employed by Turkish or international relief organizations. Still others have opened shops, grocery stores, restaurants, or barbershops in Basmane's shopping district, which, until then, was almost abandoned and run down.[6] Thanks to the recent migration wave, the street was reanimated, as an Izmir resident told me: "A few years ago, this street was totally run down, then the Syrians arrived and revitalized it."

Fluctuation in the neighborhood is huge because many Syrians sell all of their acquired belongings, sometimes even their shops, if they get the opportunity to move on. Omran spoke about his friend Bashar, who opened a small grocery shop on the Basmane shopping street shortly after his arrival: "His business went quite well. However, after two and a half years, he left last summer on a boat. Currently he is residing in Athens," he explains. "I see Arabic announcements very often that someone is leaving Izmir, searching for another Syrian to buy his shop inventory and take over the shop. They try to go on to Europe, or recently some of them have even gone back to Syria, since they do not see any prospect in Turkey."

Mohammad and Mariam, parents of two children, whom I met in May 2016, had already sold their belongings and moved on several times. Three years before, the family had left Damascus for Lebanon, then continued on to Egypt shortly thereafter. In the late autumn of 2015, they arrived in Izmir with the intention of crossing the Aegean to Europe. Mohammad quickly found a job as a cook at a Syrian restaurant in Basmane. While working to save up money for the trip, he and Mariam saw news of fatal shipwrecks and learned about the implementation of the

---

6 According to our interview partners, Syrians who want to open a shop or a restaurant in Basmane have to partner with a Turkish national, who is formally the owner of the business.

"EU–Turkey Deal" in March 2016. Eventually, the couple decided not to risk the lives of their children on a perilous boat trip, just to get stuck on a Greek island. They did not see any opportunity to move to Europe, but remaining in Turkey did not offer many prospects either. Hence they arranged a trip back to Egypt. Meanwhile, Egyptian border policies toward Syrians had changed, following the overthrow of Egyptian president Morsi (UNHCR 2014:2). To get back, they would have to be smuggled via the Sudanese–Egyptian border at a price of $4,000. Once again, they sold their belongings and gave up their work and apartment to move on. However, before departing Turkey, they realized that they had been cheated, and their money was gone, so they came back and started anew, Mohammad says in the interview. "We had to rent a new apartment, buy the necessary furniture again, and fortunately I very quickly found a new job in a restaurant." One year later, unable to move in any direction, Mohammad is saving money once again and still hoping to make it to either Europe or Egypt. He wants to leave Turkey, as living conditions there remain precarious.[7]

Omran likewise tried to establish himself during his waiting time. At first, he and some of his Syrian friends spent their time in a social center in Basmane, which tries to support migrants and refugees. In the late summer of 2016, he started to work for an international NGO in Izmir, supporting Syrians who work and live in the agricultural area surrounding Izmir. But this has not prevented him from wanting to move on. Omran tells me that his new job is a new experience, allowing him to learn new skills and to improve himself. Moreover, through his fieldwork and political engagement, he has come into contact with many different national and international NGO members, researchers, and journalists, and some of them have become his friends. This, of course, might also be of help if he manages to make it to Europe, or if he tries to establish himself in Izmir in the long term.

In almost all our interviews and conversations with Syrians in Izmir, the interview partners stressed the great importance of friendship, and of political or family networks, which extend across the whole Middle East, Europe, and beyond on different levels: psychologically, but also financially, and on the level of political activism. Migrants are sending money from Izmir to Syria, but money is also transferred the other way around. It also

---

7 Interview with Mohammad Saleh (pseudonym), Izmir, May 20, 2016 and July 10, 2016.

comes from family members in Western Europe and North America in order to pay for the boat trips to Greece, or to enable the recipient to open up a new shop in the neighborhood. Others are engaged on a political level, supporting comrades back in Syria, or, like Omran, eventually become part of an international activist network, trying to support migrants in distress in the Mediterranean Sea. The arrival of the Syrian refugees also had an influence on political activists and NGOs locally. A whole range of international and national NGOs, as well as Islamic and Christian charity organizations, have opened offices, providing support for Syrians around the district of Basmane. Furthermore, new migrant support groups, like the above-mentioned social center in Basmane, have emerged. The center hosted not only Turkish and Syrian activists, but also young foreigners from Europe, the US, and Australia, who had come to volunteer in the so-called refugee crisis in Izmir. Other already existing organizations, like the Izmir-based activist group Halkların Köprüsü (People's Bridges), orient their politics toward the needs of Syrian refugees in Izmir, and open a discussion about citizenship rights and refugees in Turkey.

In the cafés and restaurants of Basmane, Syrian politics, as well as Turkish and German migration policies, are discussed almost every day. Information about the changes within the European and Turkish migration regime is spread. Accordingly, the production of the urban space always creates a city which is not only produced locally but also outside of itself too.

## Summary

This chapter describes how the so called EU–Turkey Deal disenfranchises people and erodes the right to claim international protection even before reaching European territory. It also demonstrates how the EU–Turkey Deal has decelerated the movements of migration. The cases described show how the journeys of migrants have been hindered by the EU's pressure on Turkey regarding sea crossing toward the Greek islands and its visa policies, but also, as in Omran's case, by the Turkish state canceling its open-door policy toward Syrians. Furthermore, the cases of Mohammad and Marian illustrate the complexity of individual aspects and conditions, resulting in "fragmented" (Collyer 2010) and decelerated journeys. They initially fled to Lebanon, but the extremely precarious economic situation in which they found themselves led them to go to Egypt. Following the overthrow of President Morsi in 2013, hostility against Syrians rose in the country, leading to the exodus of many of them, like Mohammed and his family. When they arrived in Turkey, the EU–Turkey Deal stopped them from moving on to Europe, on the one hand, and on the other hand, Egypt's introduction of strict visa requirements for Syrians complicated their intention to move back to Egypt and left them waiting in Turkey, again in a precarious situation. The sense of endlessly waiting was present all over the Basmane district during our research, as the cases of the interview partners illustrate. Omran, Maya, Mohammad, and Mariam are still waiting: for their chance to move on, for a change in migration regulations, maybe for something to happen that might never happen, like Vladimir and Estragon in *Waiting for Godot*, who wait in vain. The dramatic changes in policies and practices, especially in terms of border control toward Syrian refugees, have a direct influence on migrants' experiences, movements, and orientations. They generate a feeling of being stuck in limbo.

However, the migrant movements have never stopped, as UNHCR statistics show; in August 2016, about 3,447 migrants reached the Greek islands from the Turkish mainland. Despite the reinforcement of the various borders in the region, people still manage to move on. The district of Basmane is constantly changed by the newcomers, by the people waiting and moving on, and by the traces they leave behind. Economic, political, and social spaces are produced, reproduced, and altered by incoming and remaining Syrians, who, although very often aiming to move on, engage in the urban space and enact their rights to "citizenship" by establishing new businesses, sending their children to school, and/or engaging on a political level in the urban district.

## References

AIRE Center and ECRE. 2016. "With Greece: Recommendations for Refugee Protection." June. http://www.ecre.org/wp-content/uploads/2016/07/With-Greece.pdf.

Amnesty International. 2017. "A Blueprint for Despair: Human Rights Impact of the EU–Turkey Deal." February 14. https://www.amnesty.ie/wp-content/uploads/2017/02/EU-Turkey-Deal-Briefing_Formatted_Final-P4840-3.pdf

Andersson, Ruben. 2014. "Time and the Migrant Other: European

Border Controls and the Temporal Economics of Illegality," *American Anthropologist*, 116(4): 795–805.

Antonakaki, Melina, Bernd Kasparek, and Georgios Maniatis. 2016. "Counting Heads and Channeling Bodies: The Hotspot Centre in Vial in Chios, Greece." http://transitmigration-2.org/wp-content/uploads/2016/10/ma+bk+gm--vial.hotspot.pdf

Baban, Feyzi, Suzan Ilcan, and Kim Rygiel. 2016. "Syrian Refugees in Turkey: Pathways to Precarity, Differential Inclusion, and Negotiated Citizenship Rights," *Journal of Ethnic Migration Studies*. DOI: 10.1080/1369183X.2016.1192996.

———. 2017. "Playing Border Politics with Urban Syrian Refugees." In lker Ataç, Gerda Heck, Sabine Hess, Zeynep Kasli, Philipp Ratfisch, Cavidan Soykan, and Bediz Yilmaz, eds. "Turkey's Changing Migration Regime and Its Global and Regional Dynamics." *Movements: Journal for Critical Migration and Border Regime Studies*, 3(2). https://movements-journal.org/issues/05.turkey/

Balibar, Etienne. 2003. *Sind wir Bürger Europas? Politische Integration, soziale Ausgrenzung und die Zukunft des Nationalen*. Hamburg: Hamburger Edition.

Casas-Cortes, Maribel, Sebastian Cobarrubias, Nicholas De Genova, Glenda Garelli, Giorgio Grappi, Charles Heller, Sabine Hess, et al. 2015. "New Keywords: Migration and Borders," *Cultural Studies*, 29(1): 55–87.

CJEU. 2017. Cases T-192/16, T-193/16, and T-257/16, NF, NG and NM v. European Council. 28.02.2017.

Collyer, Michael. 2010. "Stranded Migrants and the Fragmented Journey," *Journal of Refugee Studies*, 23: 1–21.

Danish Refugee Council. 2017. DRC Mixed Migration Monthly Update. April. drc.ngo

European Council. 2016. "EU-Turkey Statement." March 18. consilium.europa.eu

Gkliati, Mariana. 2017. "The EU-Turkey Deal and the Safe Third Country Concept before the Greek Asylum Appeals Committees," *Movements: Journal for Critical Migration and Border Regime Studies*, 3(2). http://movements-journal.org/issues/05.turkey/14.gkliati--eu-turkey-deal-safe-third-country-greek-asylum-appeals-committees.html.

Heck, Gerda. 2011. "'It's Been the Best Journey of My Life': Governing

# References

Migration and Strategies of Migrants at Europe's Borders: Morocco." In Mechthild Baumann, Astrid Lorenz, and Kerstin Rosenow, eds. *Crossing and Controlling Borders: Immigration Policies and Their Impact on Migrants' Journeys*, 73–86. Opladen and Farmington Hills: Budrich UniPress.

Heck, Gerda, and Sabine Hess. 2016. "European Restabilization Attempts of the External Borders and Their Consequences." HarekAct. http://harekact.bordermonitoring.eu/?s=European+Restabilization+of+the+Border+Regime

Hess, Sabine, and Bernd Kasparek, eds. 2010. *Grenzregime: Diskurse, Praktiken, Institutionen in Europa*. Berlin and Hamburg: Assoziation A.

Hess, Sabine, and Henrik Lebuhn. 2014. "Politiken der Bürgerschaft: Zur Forschungsdebatte um Migration, Stadt und Citizenship," *Sub\urban: Zeitschrift für kritische Stadtforschung*, 2(3): 11–34. http://www.zeitschrift-suburban.de/sys/index.php/suburban/article/view/153

Holston, James. 2007. *Insurgent Citizenship*. Princeton: Princeton University Press.

IOM. 2016. "Mixed Migration Flows in the Mediterranean and Beyond: Compilation of Available Data and Information: Reporting Period 2015." https://www.iom.int/sites/default/files/situation_reports/file/Mixed-Flows-Mediterranean-and-Beyond-Compilation-Overview-2015.pdf.

Isin, Engin, ed. 2008. *Recasting the Social in Citizenship*. Toronto: University of Toronto Press.

Karakayali, Serhat, and Vassilis Tsianos. 2007. "Movements that Matter." In Transit Migration Forschungsgruppe, ed. *Turbulente Ränder: Neue Perspektiven auf Migration an den Rändern Europas*, 7–22. Bielefeld: Transcript.

Kasparek, Bernd, and Sabine Hess. 2014. "Border Regime." In Nicholas De Genova, Sandro Mezzadra, and John Pickles, eds. "New Keywords: Migration and Borders," *Cultural Studies*, 29(1): 55–87.

Khosravi, Shahram. 2014. "Waiting." In B. Anderson and M. Keith, eds. *Migration: A COMPAS Anthology*. Oxford. http://compasanthology.co.uk/waiting/

Levitt, Peggy, and Nina Glick-Schiller. 2004. "Transnational Perspectives on Migration: Conceptualizing Simultaneity," *International Migration Review*, 38(45): 595–629.

Mülteci-Der and Pro Asyl. 2016. "Observations on the Situation of

Refugees in Turkey." https://www.proasyl.de/wp-content/uploads/2015/12/Mülteci-DER-OBSERVATIONS-ON-REFUGEESITUATION-TURKEY-APRIL-2016.pdf

Peers, Steve, and Emanuela Roman. 2016. "The EU, Turkey and the Refugee Crisis: What Could Possibly Go Wrong?" EU Law Analysis Blog, February 5. http://eulawanalysis.blogspot.com/2016/02/the-eu-turkey-and-refugee-crisis-what.html

Pries, Ludger. 2010. *Transnationalisierung: Theorie und Empirie grenzüberschreitender Vergesellschaftung.* Wiesbaden: VS Verlag.

Rygiel, Kim. 2010. *Globalizing Citizenship.* Vancouver: University of British Columbia Press.

Simone, AbdouMaliq. 2002. "Visible and Invisible: Remaking Cities in Africa." In Okwui Enwezor et al., eds. *Under Siege: Four African Cities: Freetown, Johannesburg, Kinshasa, Lagos.* Documenta 11, Platform 4. Ostfildern. Distributed Art Pub Incorporated.

Tazzioli, Martina. 2016. "Greece's Camps, Europe's Hotspots." Border Criminologies Blog, October 12. https://www.law.ox.ac.uk/research-subject-groups/centre-criminology/centrebordercriminologies/blog/2016/10/greece%E2%80%99s-camps

Tsianos, Vassilis, and Sabine Hess. 2010. "Ethnographische Grenzregimeanalyse: Eine Methodologie der Autonomie der Migration." In Sabine Hess and Bernd Kasparek, eds. *Grenzregime: Diskurse, Praktiken, Institutionen in Europa*, 243–264. Berlin: Assoziation A.

Ulusoy, Orçun. 2016. "Turkey as a Safe Third Country?" Border Criminologies Blog, March 29. https://www.law.ox.ac.uk/research-subject-groups/centre-criminology/centrebordercriminologies/blog/2016/03/turkey-safe-third

UNHCR. 2014. Some Improvements for Syrian Refugees in Egypt: UNHCR Egypt. https://data2.unhcr.org/en/news/13061

UNHCR. 2016a. "Regional Refugee and Migrant Response Plan for Europe." http://reporting.unhcr.org/node/13626

———. 2016b. "Refugees and Migrants Sea Arrivals in Europe." https://data2.unhcr.org/en/situations/mediterranean

Yıldız, Ayselin, and Elif Uzgören. 2016. "Limits to Temporary Protection: Non-Camp Syrian Refugees in İzmir, Turkey," *Southeast European and Black Sea Studies.* DOI: 10.1080/14683857.2016.1165492.

CHAPTER 5

# Culturalized, Gendered, and Fractured Approaches to the Integration of Refugees in Brussels

*Alexandra Parrs*

## Introduction

Recently, a project was initiated by the Belgian government to provide asylum seekers with classes on *"relations et santé sexuelle"* (relationships and sexual health) in which they would be educated on relationships and sexuality. The training material explains how to correctly greet someone in Belgium ("shake hands with a man *and* a woman") and states that it is not appropriate to "stare at a woman." A somewhat similar initiative was the creation of an online platform called Zanzu, a German–Flemish initiative developed by the Flemish Expertise Centre for Sexual Health (Sensoa) and the German Federal Center for Health Education, which aimed at explicitly teaching asylum seekers and refugees about their bodies and their sexuality. It counsels respect for women and urges creativity in sexual positions. These initiatives made it appear crucial that refugees, and, in certain cases, asylum seekers must behave appropriately in their relationships and in their sexuality in order to be integrated. Does that mean that they need to be culturally (re)educated on intimate matters to be accepted? What does it say about the assumptions concerning their culture prior to asylum or migration? And what does it say about the way receiving countries perceive their own cultural norms?

These questions inspired the reflection in this chapter, which looks at how asylum seekers and refugees are potentially educated to be better integrated in Brussels. The representations of hordes of refugees entering territories may be exacerbated in Europe because the walls, both real and symbolic, of the refugee camps are not there to serve as protection from refugees, what Agier (2008) calls "the management of the undesirables." In the absence of official refugee camps in Belgium, other symbolic barriers are erected, including reified and dichotomous identities of oppressed females and threatening males, particularly salient in the representations of refugees' sexuality, built as an embodiment of their barbarity and backwardness in direct opposition to Europeans' liberal and tolerant values. Scholars who work on the culturalization and the sexualization of citizenship note that migrants and refugees are confronted with European values that often emerge as being radically different from the values ascribed to them, particularly if they originate from Muslim and Arab countries. Tolerance is opposed to radicalism, and gender equality to patriarchal structures. Often countries reconstruct and essentialize their own liberal values in the context of migration and demand that these values become universally integrated by newcomers. Many European countries have set up different integration programs that refugees and migrants have to take to be deemed *acceptable*.

What made those questions particularly interesting is that there is an additional complexity inherent in the structure of Belgium, which is that the country is socially and culturally fractured into two administrative regions, Wallonia (French-speaking) and Flanders (Dutch-speaking). Wallonia and Flanders also have different approaches to refugees' integration, as well as different discourses on the role that culture, gender, and sexuality need to play in that process. Accordingly, the two regions have developed different integration programs for newly arrived migrants and refugees. Those programs have begun at different times, they target slightly different populations, and their content and messages differ. Further, while migrants and refugees automatically undertake the Dutch program in Flanders and the French program in Wallonia, in Belgium's capital, Brussels, they must choose between a French and a Dutch program, respectively inspired by Walloon and the Flemish ones.

In this chapter, I examine the differences between the French and Dutch integration courses' brochures available to refugees and migrants in Brussels. My goal is to understand how integration is constructed based on the different philosophies of integration (Favell 1998) prevalent in Flanders and Wallonia and how refugees are themselves perceived within the two contexts. I ask why there are two courses offered to refugees and migrants in the Brussels region rather than a single one. My analysis also relies on interviews with individuals working in the *centres d'accueil*/welcome centers in Brussels in charge of giving the courses to refugees or teaching language classes to asylum seekers. Since gender relations and sexuality appear to be crucial elements in the integration processes, I am specifically looking at the role given to culture, both migrants' and Belgian cultures, and to gender and sexuality.

## The Construction of the Refugee Identity

Much of the research on the notion of culturalization of citizenship has been conducted in the Netherlands, particularly after examining the citizenship tests that prospective migrants had to take and the naturalization movies that they had to watch (see de Leeuw and van Wichelen 2012). For Tonkens, Hurenkamp, and Duyvendak, the Dutch tend to see themselves more as a tolerant and enlightened "moral majority" (2010:236) than most nations in terms of gender equality and LGBT rights. It looks like a progressive consensus that "evidently requires policy to enforce the acculturation of those who are assumed to fall outside of it. It may come as a surprise that a progressive and tolerant country demands conformity from those whose views are not progressive" (2010:236). The writers question the impact of this monoculture on migrants' integration and see it as dualistic: on the one hand it can help Muslim migrants to question patriarchy and sexism, but, on the other, it can accentuate the value gap between the Muslim population and the majority population.

Culturalization reifies cultures—not only migrants' culture, whose backwardness is reified, but also the host country's culture, whose tolerance is reified. Often Muslim migrants and refugees are defined as culturally opposed to Christians because they have not experienced enlightenment or critical reform. They are the cultural others, and their religious practices, deemed incompatible with liberal democracy, could threaten Western societies (de Leeuw and van Wichelen 2012:201–202). Europeanness becomes an enlightened claim of moral superiority that hides the violence of its history and its own social tensions and inequalities.

Further, by employing cultural tropes of sexual freedom, gender equality, freedom of speech, and individuality as emblems of Dutchness, integration is then identified as the successful adaptation to hegemonic liberal and secular virtues, leaving little room for cultural or religious variations. The essentializing opposition between cultures (tolerant vs.

backward) is particularly salient in the citizenship tests or naturalization movies, which implicitly suggest that to be accepted as residents of the Netherlands, a political process, migrants have to demonstrate that they are culturally acceptable. Those who are excluded from that integration, the non-assimilable subjects, are identified through and against two legal political frameworks: family life and freedom of religion (de Leeuw and van Wichelen 2012:205).

Within family life, sexuality holds a central role. The sexuality of the other has long been an obsession in typical Orientalist fashion (Said 1978)—the Orientals' sexuality was scrutinized and presented as simplistically dichotomous. Males were identified as brutal and violent, and women were portrayed either as beautiful temptresses or as subordinated victims to be saved. The categorization of refugees in two opposite gendered groups followed the same model: predator males and victimized females. Much of the victimization of females is associated with sexual violence, which is indeed a representation of the reality, as in the process of conflict and refuge, women often fall victim to sexual violence and sex trafficking. However, this scrutiny of their sexuality also contributes to constructing the dichotomous roles of migrants. In Europe, since the attacks in Cologne in January 2016, all male refugees tend to be perceived as sexual predators. The refugee is often viewed as akin to the native in colonized lands (Nayar 2015:31), evaluated as being good or bad, not only already civilized but also capable of eventually being civilized—or saved from their barbaric culture. Typically, women are perceived as more salvageable because they are constructed as the victims and not the creators of the culture they belong to.

The paradox lies in the fact that while the sexuality of refugees is an obsession when it serves to portray them as either sexual predators or sexually ignorant, *their* sexuality, when not simply in contrast with *ours*, is at the same time somewhat ignored. For instance, LGBTI refugees are largely invisible and unprotected, and obtaining refugee status on the ground of sexual orientation is still a complex process. Applicants have to prove that their homosexuality is real and puts them under a well-founded fear of persecution. Discursive tolerance toward different sexual practices abounds in the European representation of itself; however, migrants are not only constructed as ignorant, but also as heterosexual, and the heterocentric framework of refugee-status determination leads only very few to question how queer migrants actually engage in the system (Gardner 2015). Further, despite its self-proclaimed interest in the well-being of refugees, the EU seems to display little practical care for their sexual and reproductive health (Finnerty 2016), including screening for cervical and breast cancer, family planning, and contraception (Keygnaert et al. 2014). The sexuality that really matters is mostly the one that serves to establish moral hierarchies or vilify refugees as dangerous rapists.

The gendered (females as vulnerable and males as threatening) and sexualized (Europeans are knowledgeable and free while migrants are ignorant and brutal) constructs illustrate a contradiction around the meaning of refugeeness. Along the road of refuge, the essence of being a refugee changes: while refugees are often first interpreted as active political actors who need to flee a country where they might be persecuted, they are then expected to gradually become passive and subdued in order to gain the right to be protected by the states where they seek refuge. There is an expectation that the refugees will be suffering bodies rather than political agents, with protection framed accordingly as a matter of sympathy and humanitarianism, rather than rights (Griffiths 2015; Fassin 2001). Therefore, in terms of expectations of who refugees are or should be, there is a shift from (perceived) masculine characteristics of resistance and fight to (perceived) feminine characteristics of vulnerability and passivity. There is a shift between who they were when they left and who they need to become when they arrive. The beliefs back home that have sometimes made the refugee become victims of persecution, and driven them to leave their country, are often discarded by the receiving country, which intends to educate refugees according to (their) correct norms and values. The fact that those values may actually be somewhat similar is almost unimaginable. As a result, the ideal refugee—political at departure, passive at arrival—is almost unattainable, as it is "so stylized and a pure figure that it is almost impossible for people to meet the constructed ideal" (Griffiths 2015:472).

## Integration Programs in Flanders and Wallonia

Belgium is a country of about 11 million inhabitants that came into existence in 1830. It is separated into two main regions, Dutch-speaking Flanders and French-speaking Wallonia, and into three linguistic communities: Dutch, French, and German. The minuscule German-speaking community is part of Wallonia and will not be studied in this chapter. While Wallonia makes up half of the area of Belgium, it hosts only one-third of its population. Flanders accounts for about half of the population, and Brussels, the capital and a region itself situated in Flanders, comprises the rest. Aside from the linguistic differences between Flanders and Wallonia, the two regions present deeply rooted differences in terms of structure and socioeconomic levels.

The two regions are also divided on the notion of migrants' integration, and there is "very little, if any, leadership by the federal government" (Martinello 2012:70) to create a consolidated approach to migrants' integration. There is very little cooperation between the two communities, particularly because the two philosophies of integration are profoundly different. According to Martinello, in Flanders a deeply engrained autonomist or even sovereignist claim has translated into sub-national laws and policies, while in Wallonia up until very recently, there was no clear vision on the issue of integration within the Walloon government (2012:70).

A concrete illustration of those differences is that while the Flemish integration program, *Inburgering*, was established more than a decade ago, Wallonia implemented a *Parcours d'intégration* only in 2013. For a decade, Wallonia seemed to resist the implementation of an integration program, and scholars have put forward a few reasons to explain its eventual development. First, the European context: since the 2010s, many European countries have set up various integration programs or citizenship tests for migrants, and a general trend of culturalization of citizenship can be noticed throughout Europe. Then, and perhaps more importantly, the Belgian context: in 2012 the Belgian law on nationality was modified to follow European trends on citizenship more closely, and a new condition for obtaining citizenship was introduced. The candidates for naturalization need to prove both their knowledge of one of the three languages of the country—French, Dutch, or German—and their social integration in Belgium. Completion of the integration program is accepted as proof of social integration (Adam 2013a), which compelled the Walloon region to implement integration programs.

Both the Flemish and the Walloon programs are designed for newly arrived migrants, specifically individuals who are foreigners, above the age of 18, legally in Belgium for less than three years, and with a residence permit of more than three months. In Flanders, however, individuals who have lived in Belgium more than three years still have to go through the program. Those exempt from the program are asylum seekers who have not yet obtained refugee status and individuals originating from another EU country. That distinction has been perceived as discriminatory by some scholars as it explicitly targets people who are not from the EU, and who are assumed to be problematic in their integration. Finally, they receive linguistic training and citizenship training; the latter is compulsory in Flanders and optional in Wallonia.[1]

## Asylum Seekers and Refugees in Brussels

In Brussels, asylum seekers and refugees represent two very distinct legal and social categories. Upon arrival in Brussels, asylum seekers can initially be hosted in one of the 80 buildings of the Federal Agency for the Reception of Asylum Seekers (Fedasil), where they live in shared spaces and are not allowed to work for four months. Fedasil operates under the supervision of the State Secretary for Asylum Policy, Migration, and Social Integration. Asylum seekers receive material support in the form of lodging and food. After four months, they can work, but in that event they need to pay a monetary contribution to their hosting facilities. Upon receiving refugee status, they can start working, if they are not already, and they have to leave the Fedasil facilities. In case of status denial, asylum seekers can appeal. Those who are permanently denied refugee status are advised to return voluntarily to the country they fled. Those who decide to stay become irregular immigrants, often akin to stateless individuals.

Recognized refugees can go through an integration program in Brussels. While new migrants and refugees arriving in Flanders or Wallonia are automatically taken care of by the region and follow the Flemish or Walloon integration policies, those in Brussels have a choice between a Dutch or a French integration program. This is, however, relatively recent, as until 2013, only the Flemish program was offered to migrants and refugees in Brussels, and it was not compulsory—therefore differing from Flanders, where it has been compulsory for the past 10 years. The French

---

1 However, there has recently been some discussion about making it compulsory in Wallonia and in the Brussels region as well.

community in Brussels did not have a French program, since there was not a program in Wallonia. In 2013, when an integration program was set up in Wallonia, it also become available in Brussels. Until 2013, refugees and migrants in Brussels did not have to enter any program, but could if they decided to do so. They had the option to take the Flemish-inspired course, offered by Brussels Onthaal Bureau (BON), "a reception agency for integration." Since the program was not compulsory, BON strived to make it particularly attractive to refugees and migrants, strategically marketing themselves by emphasizing the importance of knowing the Dutch language to ease one's integration, specifically because the knowledge of Dutch would enable newcomers to find a job more easily (Adam 2013b). The success of the Dutch program among migrants may be one of the reasons why the French community ultimately decided to set up a French-language program in 2013. In 2004, shortly after the Flemish *Inburgering* was created, there had been talk about establishing a French-language program, but it had been rejected by the socialist party that was in charge of the question of integration within the French community in Brussels at the time. Since 2004, things have changed, including the facts that many European countries have started to implement integration programs as part of their citizenship requirements and that the Belgian nationality law was modified.

In Brussels, the French-language program is offered by the French Community Commission (COCOF), an organization that takes care of the responsibilities of the French community in the Brussels-Capital Region. While the francophone parliament voted in favor of establishing an integration course in 2013, the course itself was only implemented in 2015, when the COCOF delegated the process to a few Bureaux d'Accueil pour Primo-Arrivants (BAPA), which is now in charge of the program. The program offers French language classes (240 to 700 hours) and an optional citizenship course of 50 hours (*formation à la citoyenneté*). The Dutch-language program is offered by BON, according to whom: "We offer courses on living, working, and life in Belgium and Brussels. We focus on individual counseling. BON provides specific integration programs in 18 languages. If you would rather learn Dutch as fast as possible, we'll help you with that as well." BON's Dutch program, *Inburgering*, offers Dutch classes (120 to 600 hours) and a compulsory citizenship course of 60 hours (*maatschappelijke orientatie*).

Aside from the differences in the offering agencies, the number of hours dedicated to language, and the fact that the French program has a voluntary citizenship course while the Dutch program has a compulsory one, the content of the two courses is also very different in their essence. The next section is a comparative analysis of the programs as presented in two integration brochures, from COCOF and from BON.

## The COCOF (French) Program

The 76-page COCOF brochure, "Vivre en Belgique" (2013), aims to be factual. On the topic of gender equality, it stipulates that males and females have identical rights and duties: to work and benefit from social security, vote, open a bank account, and decide where to live, how to raise children, or to divorce. The list appears to start with facts (vote, bank account) and ends with moral issues and family functions (children, divorce). The same progression, from facts to values, is discernible in another list of examples where "human dignity" is manifest (2013:11): an equal salary; social security; healthcare; social, medical, and legal support; appropriate housing; healthy environment; and cultural and social well-being (*épanouissement culturel et social*). The last items of the list are more abstract: while it is relatively easy to verify equal pay, it is far more complicated to evaluate cultural and social well-being.

The brochure explains the administrative organization of Belgium with its regions and linguistic communities, as well as administrative steps to obtain a residency permit and where to obtain documents such as passports or social security cards. It explains how to obtain a work permit, how to protect workers' rights, such as joining a union, how to obtain unemployment benefits, and how to receive additional job training. A section focuses on housing, including contractual rights and duties of renters. Another one deals with health care and medical insurance. One section addresses "couple problems and sex issues" (2013:37), and recommends seeing a doctor to obtain information about contraception, sexuality, abortion, sexually transmitted diseases, and domestic violence. The next two paragraphs (in bold green) are slightly more moralistic but remain within the realm of explicit rights: "In Belgium, a woman has the right to have children, or not, and to use contraception," and "When a woman is pregnant, she can decide to have an abortion before the 12th week of pregnancy" (2013:37).

The next section, on education, explains how to choose and apply for schools, and states that "if you have problems with language, you can go with a translator" (2013:42). A lack of knowledge in the language spoken at the school is not presented as an issue. Additionally, the language is not specified; it could be the language of the school, and not "our" national language. The text then stipulates that the only reason a school should refuse to admit a child is if the school is full, and not on the basis of whether the student has papers or not.

The next section on family begins with a Q & A: "We live together but do not want to get married. Is it possible?" The answer is "Yes, in Belgium many couples live together without being married." It then explains how to chose between a "*union libre*" or "*cohabitation légale*" (2013:48) and talks about the rights and duties of spouses, indicating that marriage does not change anything regarding the individual freedom of spouses.

The last section of the brochure focuses on "social life." The first recommendation associated with social life is to become part of an association, whether it be a cultural, philosophical, or artistic association. The brochure suggests that joining an association is a good way to "be integrated and part of cultural life" (2013:54). This carefully worded formulation appears to be a way to talk about integration without explicit mention of norms and values; the social rather than the cultural is emphasized. The rest of the text provides practical information on joining an association or being involved in different types of activities that can create social capital, such as the websites of various associations, and encouraging the newcomer to read newspapers or visit museums and libraries. Norms, values, or beliefs are deliberately absent and replaced by administrative and practical information: social integration is metaphorically embodied in a list of different associations to join, and not in cultural practices that are value-based.

## The BON (Dutch) Program

According to the Dutch BON brochure, "Migration is more than just moving from one house to another. You will be living in a country with a different language, different customs, and different laws." Unlike in the COCOF brochure, knowledge of the language is explicitly emphasized. "In Brussels, Dutch and French are the official languages," and learning Dutch is directly encouraged. "Knowledge of Dutch is a great advantage because not everyone in Brussels speaks Dutch. People who live in Brussels and speak Dutch can find a job more easily."

The BON brochure is definitely more value-based than the COCOF brochure, as it focuses, for instance, on migrants' feelings:

> *Everyone who emigrates sooner or later gets culture shock. When this happens, many migrants become withdrawn and only maintain contact with people from their own culture. But this means that the new surroundings remain strange and even threatening. The Flemish government wants to prevent this and is therefore offering you an integration program.* (2010:5)

The term "integration" is clearly used. An assessment of the migrants' feelings is made in the assumption that they will "only maintain contact with people from their own culture" and "see their surroundings as strange and threatening." The role of "prevention" by the government is also highlighted, with an assumption that without the government's intervention, things will definitely go wrong.

The brochure presents many instances of cultural tropes and direct advice: "Always respect people no matter how different they are," (2010:11) or "It is forbidden to hurt someone mentally or physically, including your partner or children" (2010:11). There is also a strong emphasis on the separation of church and state: "Everyone is free to choose his or her religion. It is forbidden to impose a religion on others" (2010:13). Employment is perceived as a key to integration: "It is very important that you look for work" (2010:15). Parents are asked to go to school meetings: "A couple of times a year, there is a parents' meeting at school. You should always attend" (2010:19).

A similar culturalist discourse is visible in the area of marriage: "If you are coming to Flanders to marry, you should bear in mind that your expectations about the relationship may be different from your partner's. You should think about this and discuss it with your partner." Finally, the advice on "living together in a pleasant environment" suggests that people know their neighbors, but respect the fact that "Flemish people like peace and quiet," and they like "their privacy" (2010:29). This advice seems to assume that all Flemish people enjoy peace, quiet, and privacy, and all non-Flemish will be loud and intrusive. How intrinsic characteristics of one people are chosen (being quiet) is very telling about what is expected from the others (being loud). The prevention of the loudness is constructed by manufacturing it as "un-Flemish." In the same vein, another item on "living with family" mentions that adult sons and daughters move out of their parents' home in Belgium, a narrative in opposition to the assumption that many of the newcomers live otherwise.

**Facts and Norms**

One of the main differences between the two approaches explicitly identifiable in the brochures is COCOF's emphasis on how Belgium functions with its institutions and explicit rules politically anchored, and BON's emphasis on implicit norms and values culturally anchored. BON's approach is clearly embedded in the discourse of culturalization of citizenship, which in Western European societies denotes the increasing importance attached to culture and morality in shaping citizenship and integration policy (Geschiere 2009; Tonkens et al. 2010; de Leeuw and van Wichelen 2012). Values and norms are essentialized and presented as absolute, covering up potential tensions or divisions within Belgian society—including the very dissension between the two regions, or the fact that there are still many issues in the realms of gender equality in Belgium, specifically with respect to labor, household tasks, or childcare.

These approaches also reflect different trends within Europe. Countries that emphasize the cultural aspect of integration also typically politicize integration more explicitly, constructing it as a threat against national values that can be controlled only by a stronger assimilation of migrants (Adam 2013a; Bale 2003; Schain 2006). The Flemish region is more in line with the right-wing discourse of culturalization of citizenship and cultural integration. On the contrary, Wallonia and French-speaking Brussels seem to be positioned in opposition to other more restrictive European countries that have succumbed to populism. It is worth noting that unlike many of its neighbors, the Walloon region and Brussels are situated less to the right of the political spectrum and there is no far-right party in the Walloon region, unlike in Flanders. This also means that other parties are less inclined to support nationalistic discourses in order to lure votes away from a far-right party. According to Bocker and Strik, it is the absence of far-right parties that has saved the Walloon region from nationalistic/cultural integration discourses (2011). What is interesting is that two very different philosophies of integration are cohabiting within the same nation; their geographical proximity thus permits a rather accurate comparison of the philosophies and how these philosophies affect migration policies.

The two distinct approaches symbolize differences in philosophies of integration and awarding of citizenship between Dutch- and French-speaking Belgium, but also differences in the role of educating migrants and refugees about their new country and how this education should be implemented. The French brochure approaches education as a process that should allow migrants to obtain the same services in terms of employment and health care, and in that sense the focus is on creating equal access to practical knowledge about how these services work. In the Dutch approach, the goal of the educational process is to allow migrants to understand new cultural norms in order to navigate society and fit in better—a more culturalist approach.

While the approaches of the Walloon and French communities in Brussels do not focus on norms and try to remain neutral in terms of gender and sexuality, the Flemish culturalizing initiative gives them a central role: gender and sexuality belong to the realm of culture. Not only is gender discussed explicitly in the BON brochure, but additional initiatives have given gender and sexuality a central position on the path to cultural integration. One of these initiatives is the website Zanzu mentioned in the introduction. Zanzu targets migrants and refugees, but also asylum seekers. It addresses questions of sexuality via a series of drawings explicitly illustrating sexual relations, including heterosexual, homosexual, and interracial. The goal of the site is to teach the viewers how to have sex and to explore new ways to do so, in a sort of sexualization of citizenship, or at least a sexualization of belonging. While these are topics worth raising for everyone, Zanzu's narrative seems to assume that refugees come from cultures and backgrounds that intrinsically embrace violence toward women and LGBTI individuals. It also conveniently ignores how issues like virginity and hymen worship plague women in Western culture. It appears to be largely based on the image of a unified Arab culture, incapable of respecting women and constantly trying to subjugate them (Libera 2016:23).

## Regional Opposition and Competition

The two approaches are not only emblematic of differences in terms of philosophy of integration, and cultural and educational goals, but they also appear to be the manifestation of the more overarching opposition between the two regions. Possibly the presence of a different philosophy of integration in the neighboring regions contributes to reification of each region's position as intrinsically different from its neighbor. In other words, the COCOF approach almost seems to be constructing itself as not being culturalizing, as not being Flemish, as being purposefully different—more tolerant. Ironically, the concept of tolerance is appropriated by both sides. Tolerance can embody enlightened views in terms of gender equality and sexual practices, and in that context is opposed to the migrants' assumed patriarchy, which is largely detectable in the Flemish narrative. On the other hand, the Walloon approach is to manifest tolerance in refusing to succumb to a cultural imperialist approach toward migrants by carefully avoiding the imposition of its norms and values. The presence of refugees and migrants and their management seems to become a factor that serves to crystallize the philosophical differences in terms of identity between the two communities. In that sense, migrants become the unsuspecting catalysts of the further reification of two identities in conflict and competition.

An article published in July 2016 by the ASBL[2] Coordination et Initiatives pour Réfugiés et Étrangers (CIRE) offers some reflections on the francophone program in Brussels. It identifies differences with the Flemish program. For instance, the Walloon/Brussels program, despite some differences, is based on philosophies that perceive migration as a process by which both migrants and the host society are transformed, which is in opposition with the culturalization that implies that only migrants are transformed to adapt to the host society: "It is important to allow for interactions between native populations and migrants and to engage each to discover the other's culture." The article also remarks that the Walloon/francophone Brussels programs "came late," which explains why they are developed in relation—mostly in opposition but also in competition—to the Flemish and BON programs.

---

2 *Association sans but lucratif*: not-for profit organization.

Local language learning is an interesting illustration of the complexities of the relationship between the programs. The BON brochure clearly emphasizes the usefulness of Dutch to find employment: "People who live in Brussels and speak Dutch can find a job more easily." The COCOF brochure does not mention learning French and suggests that if a child's parents do not speak French, this should not prevent the child from attending school because parents can be provided with a translator. The BON brochure implies that mastering the language, specifically Dutch, is key to integration; the COCOF suggests that not mastering the language (and no language is specified) should not be a deterrent to integration. Despite that discourse, however, the COCOF program offers more hours of language than the BON. Further, language is more strongly emphasized in the francophone program in Brussels than in the Walloon program (Adam 2013a), which may be explained by the competition that is unquestionably present between the two programs and the fact that the BON program has been advocating for years for the importance of teaching Dutch to migrants. Both philosophical and practical considerations can be identified.

Vocabulary is also a point of contention. While the Flemish program has always wholeheartedly used the term 'integration,' the Walloon program has only recently begun to speak about 'integration,' and the COCOF francophone program in Brussels only talks about *'accueil'* (welcome), perceived as less culturally imposing. The decision to use 'integration' or *'accueil'* is symbolic of the fracture in terms of discourse, not only among regions, but also within civil society. While some association representatives I spoke with favor *'accueil,'* other interlocutors preferred 'integration,' arguing that it was pointless to hide the reality and "to be scared of words," as integration was "[what was] needed and people dealing with migrants need to be braver."

Another noticeable point of opposition is that the COCOF program strives to be more flexible (CIRE 2016) than the BON one, and its brochure is more of a guideline that can serve to promote the course. There is more space for the providers of the course, the BAPAs as well as the associations who use the COCOF brochure, to interpret it, and those different interpretations are sometimes in conflict. Interlocutors at one of the BAFAs explained that most associations had tailored the courses for the refugees according to their own visions. They strived to be factual and not value- or norm-based. When I asked how gender was discussed, one interlocutor answered:

> *We never have direct teachings about women. We start discussions about other things and if there is a gender component, then we address it. For instance when we talk about voting rights, or political rights, we end up talking about gender, women voting and so on, but not directly. We don't preach. We have discussions.*

When I asked whether his organization would use the material developed for the classes on *"relations et santé sexuelle"* that are supposed to be given to asylum seekers and refugees, he answered negatively. According to other interlocutors in French-speaking associations, it is not (yet) compulsory for them to give refugees and asylum seekers these classes, but it may be in the Fedasil Center —there are a lot of uncertainties on this point and no one was able to confirm it. However, another interlocutor in charge of the citizenship course mentioned that in her association they refused to "avoid talking about gender." She then explained that many others used the discourse of cultural relativism to avoid challenging patriarchal and other unacceptable practices, but her association did not. "We talk about male domination and things like that and we don't care if people say we are not culturally sensitive, as this cultural sensitivity enables the oppression of women. But not here."

There are clearly different approaches in French-speaking Brussels, and while there is uniform rejection of the more imposing Flemish approach, divergences remain in whether to address gender issues directly or not. Pristed Nielsen's 2013 analysis is insightful: it suggests that in Europe, feminists and antiracists tend to clash in the area of discrimination. She builds her reflection on Crenshaw's point that the failure of feminism to interrogate race means that resistance strategies of feminism will often replicate and reinforce the subordination of people of color, and concomitantly, the failure of antiracism to interrogate patriarchy means that antiracism will frequently reproduce the subordination of women (1991). She wonders whether feminism and antiracism can jointly fight discrimination in Europe: can they be appropriated wrongly by other parties (feminists and gays by right-wing parties, for instance, to critique Islamic patriarchy), or will antiracists forget gender inequality in the name of cultural relativism and cultural differences in terms of gender? Can the different actors resist the "hierarchy of oppression" (racial or gender—which is higher on the agenda?), and can there be an intersectional approach—real, not just theoretical? Many members of the relevant associations seem to be struggling with these questions.

## Conclusion

Many questions are raised by the structure of these two integration programs. First, we can ask to what extent these programs actually address gender inequalities among refugees, or if, instead, they serve to reify boundaries between refugees and non-refugees by condescendingly opposing the liberal and tolerant Europeans to uneducated and essentially patriarchal migrants. The programs are also tools to erect boundaries between the two Belgian regions by opposing visions of integration and belonging, one being more norm-based and the other trying to be embedded in equality of knowledge between citizens and newly arrived migrants. Different terms are appropriated to define strategies and identities, such as tolerance, which can be defined as the opposite of patriarchal values or cultural imperialism.

My analysis reveals how these programs act to create additional distance between refugees and citizens and also serve as a political discourse to embody the Flemish and Walloon differences in approach to refugee integration. The gendered discourse on refugees does not necessarily have refugees' well-being as its main goal. Rather, this discourse is politicized and reflects more the sentiments and contradictions of Belgian society itself, in terms of its own divisions and in terms of its relationship to the 'others' (particularly refugees). As a result, these two integration initiatives are fragmented instead of encompassing or intersectional, both in terms of regional differences and in terms of approaches. These fractures create a constellation of ideas and approaches when they probably would benefit from more cooperation between the different regions, as well as between social actors.

## References

Adam, I. 2013a. "Immigrant Integration Policies of the Belgian Regions: Sub-State Nationalism and Policy Divergence after Devolution," *Regional and Federal Studies*, 23(5): 547–569.

———. 2013b. "Pourquoi un parcours d'accueil pour primo-arrivants voit-il le jour à Bruxelles aujourd'hui?" Conseil Bruxellois de Coordination Sociopolitique (CBCS). http://www.cbcs.be/Pourquoi-un-parcours-d-accueil

Agier, M. 2008. *On the Margins of the World: The Refugee Experience Today*. Cambridge: Polity Press.

Bale, T. 2003. "Cinderella and Her Ugly Sisters: The Mainstream and Extreme Right in Europe's Bipolarising Party Systems," *West European Politics*, 26(3): 67–90.

Bocker, A., and T. Strik. 2011. "Language and Knowledge Tests for Permanent Residence Rights: Help or Hindrance for Integration?" *European Journal of Migration and Law*, 13(2): 157–184.

CIRE. 2016. *Rapport annuel pour l'année 2016*.

Crenshaw, K. 1991. "Mapping the Margins: Intersectionality, Identity Politics, and Violence Against Women of Color," *Stanford Law Review*, 43(6): 1241–1299.

COCOF. 2013. Vivre en Belgique. https://www.spfb.brussels/sites/default/files/documents/guide-nouveaux-arrivants-belgique-bruxelles-wallonie_fr.pdf

De Leeuw, M., and S. van Wichelen. 2012. "Civilizing Migrants: Integration, Culture and Citizenship," *European Journal of Cultural Studies*, 15(2): 195–210.

Fassin, D. 2001. "The Biopolitics of Otherness: Undocumented Foreigners and Racial Discrimination in French Public Debate," *Anthropology Today*, 17: 3–7.

Favell, A. 1998. *Philosophies of Integration: Immigration and the Idea of Citizenship in France and Britain*. New York: St. Martin's Press.

Finnerty, F. 2016. "Sexual and Reproductive Health in the New Migrant 'Jungle' Camp in Calais, France: A Perfect Storm?" http://blogs.bmj.com/sti/2016/01/29/sexual-and-reproductive-health-in-the-new-migrant-jungle-camp-in-calais-france-a-perfect-storm/?utm_source=TrendMD&utm_medium=cpc&utm_campaign=STI_blog_TrendMD-0

Gardner, J. L. 2015. "(In)credibly Queer: Sexuality-Based Asylum in the European Union." In Anthony Chase and Judith S. Goldstein, eds. *Transatlantic Perspectives on Diplomacy and Diversity*, 39–66. New York: Humanity in Action Press.

# References

Geschiere, P. 2009. *The Perils of Belonging: Autochthony, Citizenship, and Exclusion in Africa and Europe*. Chicago, IL: University of Chicago Press.

Griffiths, M. 2015. "'Here, Man Is Nothing!' Gender and Policy in an Asylum Context," *Men and Masculinities*, 18(4): 468–488.

Inburgering. 2010. Migration to Flanders. https://www.integratie-inburgering.be/sites/default/files/atoms/files/brochure_engels.pdf

Keygnaert, I., A. Guieu, G. Ooms, N. Vettenburg, M. Temmerman, and K. Roelens. 2014. "Sexual and Reproductive Health of Migrants: Does the EU Care?" *Health Policy*, 114(2–3): 215–225.

Libera, M. D. 2016. "Sex with the Other: Anxieties and Representations of Gender in Europe during the Refugee Crisis," *International Journal of Multicultural and Multireligious Understanding*, 3(6): 19–29.

Martinello, M. 2012. "Belgium." In Christian Joppke and F. Leslie Seidle, eds. *Immigrant Integration in Federal Countries*, 58–79. Montreal and Kingston: McGill-Queen's University Press.

Nayar, P. K. 2015. *The Postcolonial Studies Dictionary*. Chichester, UK: Wiley Blackwell.

Pristed Nielsen, H. 2013. "Joint Purpose? Intersectionality in the Hands of Anti-Racist and Gender-Equality Activists in Europe," *Ethnicities*, 13(3): 276–294.

Said, E. 1978. *Orientalism*. New York: Pantheon.

Schain, M. A. 2006. "The Extreme-Right and Immigration Policy-Making: Measuring Direct and Indirect Effects," *West European Politics*, 29(2): 270–289.

Tonkens, E., M. Hurenkamp, and J. W. Duyvendak. 2010. "Culturalization of Citizenship in the Netherlands." In Ariane Chebel d'Appollonia and Simon Reich, eds. *Managing Ethnic Diversity after 9/11: Integration, Security, and Civil Liberties in Transatlantic Perspective*, 233–252. New Brunswick, NJ: Rutgers University Press.

CHAPTER 6

# Diaspora Politics in Illiberal Contexts: Authoritarianism and Cross-Border Mobility in the Modern Middle East

*Gerasimos Tsourapas*

## Introduction

"There has been an amazing explosion [in turnout as] around 1.42 million votes have been cast," Turkish president Tayyip Erdoğan jubilantly declared in the aftermath of Turkey's April 2017 referendum (Gumrukcu 2017).[1] He was not referring to domestic election results, but to the turnout of Turks living abroad. In fact, Erdoğan considered the diaspora vote so important that he did not hesitate to enter into diplomatic imbroglios with a number of European states: when state authorities refused to allow political campaigns to be staged in the Netherlands, Erdogan called the Dutch "fascists" and "Nazi remnants," threatening diplomatic and economic retaliations (Koinova 2017). The international dimension of the 2017 Turkish referendum brings to the forefront a key aspect of politics that has yet to be sufficiently theorized in a comparative manner, namely the engagement of Middle Eastern states with their populations abroad. In this chapter, I demonstrate how authoritarian emigration states in the Middle East typically develop multi-tier policies that target different stages of mobility: *exit* policies regulate the emigration of citizens; *diaspora* policies target those residing outside the borders of the nation-state; finally, *return* policies manage their potential re-entry into the nation-state.[2]

---

1  I am grateful for the generous support of Iman A. Hamdy in drafting this chapter, as well as the constructive feedback provided by Professor Ibrahim Awad. The chapter is based on an earlier research paper; see Tsourapas 2018c.

2  It bears mentioning that I am focusing on such policies with regard to mobility measures only, and do not specifically address other policy measures that aim to maximize remittances, promote investments, or protect diasporas.

## Introduction

States' outreach policies toward their diasporas have become a global phenomenon (Délano 2014; Adamson 2016), with the majority of states developing a range of diverse policies that go beyond mere consular support for expatriates. A growing number of states are implementing out-of-country voting processes (Caramani and Grotz 2015), dual-citizenship provisions (Mirilovic 2014; Blatter 2011), and a variety of other policies that aim to strengthen connections to the homeland (Gamlen 2014; Brinkerhoff 2008). A sizable body of literature has built on archetypical cases of democracies' development of migration and diaspora institutions—namely India (Varadarajan 2010; Naujoks 2013), Mexico (Fitzgerald 2009; Délano 2011), and the Philippines (Guevarra 2009; Rodriguez 2010). Over the past few years, political scientists have been identifying how autocracies also target those residing outside the boundaries of the nation-state. An emerging literature identifies the development of diaspora engagement policies in China (Smart and Hsu 2004), Russia (King and Melvin 2006), Latin America (Margheritis 2015), and elsewhere. Despite a few exceptions (see recent work by Koinova 2018; Adamson 2018), there exists an assumption that states develop a unitary diaspora policy, targeting all groups abroad in a similar manner. In contrast to the diaspora literature on liberal democracies or democratizing states, the full range of mechanisms that "authoritarian emigration states" may develop remains underexamined.[3] While researchers acknowledge that regime type matters (Koinova and Tsourapas 2018), the majority of work in this field is dominated by single case studies (Natter 2015; Tsourapas 2016; Smart and Hsu 2004; Hirt and Mohammad 2017).[4] Do non-democracies develop identical sets of diaspora engagement policies as liberal democracies and, if not, do they face additional constraints or opportunities? Ultimately, what is the range of policies developed by authoritarian emigration states?

In order to address these questions and stimulate further comparative research on state–diaspora policies in the global South, I examine

---

3 Drawing on Hollifield's work on migration states and Gamlen's work on emigration states (Hollifield 2004; Gamlen 2008), I define authoritarian emigration states as "the set of institutions, practices, and mechanisms regulating cross-border mobility developed within non-democratic contexts" (for a full discussion, see Tsourapas 2018a).

4 Notable exceptions include Mirilovic (2014) and Brand (2006).

the various ways in which states in the Middle East attempt to engage with their population groups abroad. In contrast to the expectations of the literature for unitary, homogenous diaspora policies, I build on earlier research to argue that authoritarian emigration states develop multi-tier emigrant policies (Tsourapas 2015b), and that they engage with emigrants in three separate stages of their mobility. Firstly, policies of *exit* regulate aspects related to emigration from the country of origin; secondly, *diaspora* policies target population groups beyond the territorial boundaries of the nation-state; finally, *return* policies set processes of readmission into the country of origin. To illustrate these multi-tier emigrant policies in practice, I draw from the long tradition of diverse flows of migration in the region. While I do not expect to create a comprehensive typology of the range of non-democracies' diaspora policies, I aim to problematize existing conceptualizations of (frequently unitary) state–diaspora relations that are based upon liberal democracies.

The chapter proceeds as follows: I begin by examining the literature on state–diaspora relations more closely, and I identify a gap in the diverse ways in which authoritarian emigration states attempt to reach out to their populations abroad. I continue by arguing for a multi-tier approach to state–diaspora relations in non-democratic contexts, before proceeding to examine the policies of five Middle Eastern states—Libya, Syria, Egypt, Turkey, and Jordan—in the 1970–2010 period. In each case, I identify how the state developed multi-tiered emigrant policies, often targeting distinct population groups in different manners. I conclude with a discussion of how the chapter's argumentation and theoretical focus may be carried forward in the future.

## Diaspora Policy-Making and the Authoritarian Emigration State

This section examines how scholars have approached the question of autocracies' policies toward their diasporas, or their populations abroad. It highlights two important gaps, namely with regard to the under-theorization of states' emigration and return migration policies and the wide variations in policies developed by these states. Political scientists have traditionally approached autocracies as aiming to restrict their citizens' cross-border mobility and prevent emigration at any cost (Alemán and Woods 2014). This was a Cold War perspective shaped by the construction of the Berlin Wall and the German Democratic Republic's shoot-to-kill policy toward anyone attempting to cross it. With the 'transnational turn' in international relations over the last 20 years, scholars shifted their attention to diaspora policies, gradually beginning to theorize as to the conditions under which emigration states reached out to their communities abroad (Collyer 2013; Gamlen 2008). The focus of this early strand of literature was predominantly on liberal democracies, leaving an 'extraterritorial gap' in studies of autocratic politics (Glasius 2017). Over the past few years, a new wave of scholars have drawn their theoretical underpinnings from the diaspora literature to theorize on how autocracies also develop similar policies (Koinova and Tsourapas 2018). These countries seek to engage with their migrant and diaspora communities (De Haas 2007); some introduce out-of-country voting processes (Brand 2014); others may also target citizens abroad for specific purposes, be they material (Escribà-Folch, Meseguer, and Wright 2015; Iskander 2010), political (Moss 2016; Tsourapas 2016), or both (Brand 2006; Hirt and Mohammad 2017; Tsourapas 2015b).

Yet the importation of state–diaspora relations models developed within liberal democratic frameworks into an authoritarian context faces two analytical hurdles. Firstly, autocracies, by definition, seek to exert a greater degree of control throughout citizens' migration trajectory. 'Inclusive' diaspora policies developed by democracies do not travel as easily in autocratic contexts that do not share liberal understandings of citizenship, membership, or rights (cf. Glasius 2017). More concretely in terms of mobility, Article 13b of the Universal Declaration of Human Rights ("Everyone has the right to leave any country, including his own, and to return to his country") has been challenged by many non-democracies that do not regard cross-border mobility as a right. Empirical work has highlighted how autocracies seek to manipulate the size and well-being of their diasporas by regulating citizens' exit, return, or both—corresponding to a small group of scholars who are beginning to trace the linkages between emigration and return migration in states' diaspora policies (Markowitz and Stefansson 2004; Mylonas 2013; Tsourapas 2015b), or their citizenship laws (Leblang 2011). At the same time, diasporas also constitute an object of contention and diplomatic negotiation between individual states, or of states' migration diplomacy (Tsourapas 2017).

Thus, beyond policies that exclusively target those populations already residing outside their borders, non-democracies develop two additional sets of policies in order to control the size and makeup of their diasporas. Firstly, they regulate their citizens' emigration processes to a much greater extent than liberal democracies do. For citizens aiming to emigrate from Uzbekistan or North Korea, for example, exit visas continue to remain a strict requirement. Particularly in previous decades, 'black lists' identified citizens, usually political dissenters, who were specifically prohibited from emigrating. Secondly, they regulate their citizens' return migration processes. Autocracies may complicate the process of return migration by not allowing dual citizenship or by unilaterally stripping political dissenters of their nationality. This is particularly popular across the Gulf states ("To Silence Dissidents" 2016). Qatar revoked the citizenship of an entire clan, approximately 6,000 members of the al-Ghufran branch of the al-Murrah tribe, in 2004–2005 because of lack of loyalty to the emir (Parolin 2009). In even more extreme cases, a number of autocracies have also not hesitated to diminish their 'opposition in exile' through forced extraditions, as in Central Asia (Cooley and Heathershaw 2017), or even to engage in political assassinations, as in the case of Russia under Putin. States, in Adamson's apt characterization, are able to both "generate" and "shape" diasporas (Adamson 2018); in autocratic contexts, they also appear able to "dismantle" them.

## Theorizing State–Diaspora Relations in the Middle East

Based on the aforementioned empirical observations regarding non-democracies' policies toward cross-border population mobility, the chapter's first hypothesis is that authoritarian emigration states typically develop multi-tier policies aimed at three separate stages of cross-border mobility: *exit*, *diaspora*, and *return* (table 1).

**Libyan emigrant policies.** Oil-rich Libya is traditionally regarded as a country of immigration or, more recently, transit migration (Bredeloup and Pliez 2011; Paoletti 2011; Tsourapas 2017). But while emigration flows never reached the high figures of other Middle Eastern and African states, Libya experienced sustained labor emigration, particularly temporary emigration of students and high-skilled professionals, dispersed across multiple host states. Short-term emigration can be explained primarily from a developmental perspective: King Idris, the

## Theorizing State–Diaspora Relations in the Middle East

**Table 1. Authoritarian emigration states and cross-border mobility**

| Policy tier | Policy examples |
|---|---|
| Exit | Legal regulations regarding the issuance of travel documents<br>Existence of 'black lists' to prevent select individuals' cross-border mobility<br>Informal processes facilitating, or hindering, emigration and/or return migration<br>Restrictions on travel based on age, sex, occupation, fulfillment of military service obligations, or criminal record<br>Bilateral agreements with (potential) countries of destination |
| Diaspora | Centralized decision-making on diaspora policy across a small number of domestic institutional actors<br>Consular support for diaspora-related activities<br>Monitoring or surveillance of population groups' activities; attempts at intimidation or corporal punishment<br>Attempts at financial extraction, through taxation or other means<br>Out-of-country voting provisions<br>Targeting of family and friends back in the homeland |
| Return | Provisions on dual/multiple citizenship<br>Practices of denationalization<br>Arrest upon re-entry<br>Forced extradition processes<br>Development of 'black lists' preventing return migration |

first ruler of post-independence Libya (1951–1969), relied on foreign staff to develop the Libyan state and train Libyan citizens (Vandewalle 2012; Tsourapas 2015a), but his successor, Muammar Gaddafi, encouraged the emigration of Libyans for skill-acquisition purposes instead. Political scientists have examined how Libyan elites have manipulated the status of the country both as a transit and as a host country of migrants for economic and foreign policy gains in its migration diplomacy (Greenhill 2010; Tsourapas 2017), yet little has been written on the country's complex emigrant policy.

With regard to managing emigration through the state's exit policy, Libya under Gaddafi regulated emigration almost to the point of restriction. At the time, the ruling regime considered a Libyan's relocation abroad to constitute a political act hostile to the state, and duly developed a variety of repressive mechanisms to prevent this: for decades, Libya practiced a rigid system of 'exit visa' regulations for Libyan nationals. The issuance of travel documents was also extremely complex, involving a number of bureaucratic and administrative channels. Requests for an exit visa were likely to be unsuccessful, or result in imprisonment, if one had been placed on one of the regime's 'black lists' merely for being a friend or relative of another Libyan abroad. In the 2004 case of *Loubna El Ghar v. Socialist People's Libyan Arab Jamahiriya*, the UNHRC determined that Libya refused the issuance of a passport "without any valid justification and subjected [her] to an unreasonable delay, and as a result . . . prevented [her] from travelling abroad to continue her studies." The state also imposed heavy penalties on those who attempted to emigrate without proper permission, while the facilitation of unauthorized emigration carried both a prison penalty and a fine, as formalized in Law No. 2/2004 and Law No. 19/2010.

Libya also developed an extensive diaspora policy that sought to extend control over Libyans' activities abroad. This included efforts to mobilize Libyan students against potential anti-regime activists organized by Omar Sodani in the 1980s. More frequently, the Gaddafi regime would paint these migrant and diaspora groups as traitors to the Libyan state or, more frequently, *killab dala* ('stray dogs'), promising vengeance. In his 1982 "Day of Vengeance" speech, Gaddafi made particular mention of these political dissenters: "these stray dogs composed of ex-premiers who are traitors and hirelings. They demean the Libyan people because they sold out Libya. . . . There shall be no mercy for the agents of America. The escaped hirelings, enemies of the Libyan people, shall not escape from this people." In the Libyan case, patriotism and loyalty to the regime entailed a rejection of the West (cf. Shain 2005), and thus emigration was politically suspect. Pargeter recounts:

> *Teams of rough and ready revolutionaries moved in and took over the Libyan embassies (now named "people's bureaus") around the world and began rooting out the "stray dogs" who were engaged in anti-regime*

*activities. Eliminating the opposition was far more important to Qaddafi than the niceties of foreign diplomacy.* (Pargeter 2012:103–104)

Libyan strategies of silencing the diaspora included political assassinations. Many of these campaigns were reportedly spearheaded by Moussa Koussa, nicknamed *mab'uth al-mawt* ('envoy of death'). In 1980, Koussa was formally removed from his position as public envoy in London when he publicly admitted these practices to the London *Times*: "We killed two in London and there were another two to be killed. . . . I approve of this" (*The Times*, June 11, 1980). Earlier in May, the assassin of Salem Fezzani, a Libyan living in Italy shot dead in his restaurant in Rome, declared "I was sent by the people to kill him. He is a traitor and an enemy of the people" (quoted in Pargeter 2012:105). Many dissidents mysteriously disappeared, such as Mansour Rashid el-Kikhia, minister of foreign affairs from 1972 to 1973. Having disagreed with Gaddafi's policies, el-Kikhia was granted American citizenship and went on to help found the Arab Organization of Human Rights. He disappeared in Cairo in 1993, and his remains were only discovered in Libya in 2012. As Salem al-Hassi, Libya's intelligence chief following the Arab Spring (2012–2015), recounts:

*I was not the only one who was pursued by the Gaddafi intelligence services. For years, the Gaddafi intelligence services went after opposition leaders in the capitals of many countries, in Europe, the United States, and Arab countries. A great number of opposition leaders were handed over to Gaddafi by Arab and European countries. A great number were kidnapped in Arab and European countries. The regime used the most evil ways to eliminate the opposition.* (quoted in *Asharq al-Awsat* 2012)

Finally, beyond trying to control diasporic activity by targeting Libyans who wished to exit and those who resided abroad, the Gaddafi regime also tailored its return diaspora policy to accomplish similar aims. The US Department of State noted in a 1994 report:

*The Revolutionary Committees maintain surveillance of some Libyans while they are abroad. Libyan nationals' right of return is*

> *theoretically fully protected, even for opponents of General Qadhafi. However, this "right" may be more nearly an obligation; the regime often calls on students, many of whom receive a government subsidy, and others working abroad to return on little or no notice and without regard to the impact on their studies or work. Libyans who study abroad are interrogated on their return home. A number of Libyans, including most exiled opposition leaders, refuse to return.* (US Department of State 1994)

At the same time, the regime would attempt to force Libyan dissenters to return to the homeland in order to face persecution and appropriate punishment. The intended aim was to dissuade Libyans from emigrating by highlighting the risks involved. Not surprisingly, the regime's treatment of return migrants often involved public show trials. One of the most chilling was the case of al-Sadek Hamed al-Shuwehdy, who had emigrated to pursue an engineering degree in the US. He was publicly executed in 1984, in the middle of a stadium full of thousands of schoolchildren and students, who had been brought in for the occasion. After he tearfully confessed to having joined the 'stray dogs,' a gallows was brought into the arena and al-Shuwedhy was hanged, on live television.

While such events were also aimed at dissuading any Libyan exiles from returning to the homeland, the state's emigrant policy also developed a rigid legal framework for restricting any attempts at repatriation: for one, dual citizenship was expressly forbidden by Nationality Law No. 17/1954 and Law No. 3/1979. At the same time, a common measure adopted for political dissenters abroad, or those who had emigrated without formal permission, was denaturalization. Libya had introduced detailed regulations for the process of involuntary loss of Libyan citizenship on the following grounds:

> *Person obtains new citizenship without government permission. Person enlists in foreign military or attempts to avoid Libyan conscription. Person seeks asylum in another country. Person attempts to smuggle money out of the country. Person converts to a religion other than Islam. Person deserted country after 1969 revolution. Person refuses to return home within 6 months of state request. Person commits treasonous acts*

*against the state. Additional grounds for a naturalized citizen: Person commits crimes against the security of the state. Person remains outside the country for more than two years. Person obtained citizenship through fraud or false statement.* (Tsourapas, 2018c)

**Syrian emigrant policies.** Like Libya, the Syrian Arab Republic, or Syria, has traditionally been regarded as an authoritarian emigration state, given the numerous restrictions that the Assad regime placed on population mobility (Philipp 1985; Winckler 1997). Yet Syria has experienced waves of low-skilled emigration into Lebanon for decades (Chalcraft 2008), as well as into the Gulf countries from the mid 1970s onward. Similar to the Libyan case, Syrians also fled the political regime of Hafez al-Assad by emigrating to the West, particularly during the 1980s, which saw a wave of harsh repression.

In terms of Syria's exit policy, low-skilled Syrians were able to pursue short-term labor emigration into Lebanon and oil-producing Arab states. This was supervised by the regime via bilateral accords with the Arab host states and is best understood as a 'safety valve' process that allowed low-skilled, unemployed Syrians the opportunity to pursue temporary or cyclical employment in neighboring states. Yet the process for emigrating elsewhere was deliberately cumbersome, put in place by a regime keen on "preventing the migration of skilled and professional workers by means of coercion and by denying exit visas to those who were important to the economy" (Winckler 1997:113). As in Libya, the regime did not allow free emigration, instituting a rigid process for exit visas. Irregular exit, without proper documentation, was punishable by three months in prison and/or a fine of 500 Syrian pounds, according to Law No. 42/1975. Relatives of those who had emigrated without permission, or who were politically active abroad, also faced restrictions on movement. Public-sector employees, in particular, were expressly forbidden from seeking employment abroad without a permit. In order to prevent the emigration of high-skilled Syrians, the state introduced a law in 1988 stating that anyone graduating with an engineering degree, and unable to find work in the private sector, would be employed in the public sector for at least five years.

At the same time, the Assad regime's diaspora policy targeted many Syrian groups abroad in a manner reminiscent of the Libyan state strategies. Numerous reports on 'disappearances' of Syrians abroad exist. Political dissenters abroad have also been victims of assassinations. Muhammad Umran, a founding member of the Ba'th Party, was imprisoned following the 1966 Syrian coup d'état; he fled to Lebanon upon his release, where he was assassinated in March 1972. Salah ad-Din al-Bitar, another founder of the Ba'th Party and later prime minister of Syria, fled to Europe in 1966 and was killed in July 1980 in Paris, after calling for the overthrow of Assad. In response, Assad announced only four days after al-Bitar's assassination that "all those who oppose the regime will be annihilated.... We will pursue them everywhere." In order to suppress any political activism beyond the national borders, the Syrian regime has developed an elaborate web of diaspora policies that combine monitoring, intimidation, and active repression of population groups abroad (Moss 2016).

Finally, the Syrian regime developed return policies reminiscent of Libya. Dual nationality requires authorization from the Syrian authorities, and there are legal sanctions against the acquisition of a second nationality without authorization. Among other conditions, such authorization is expressly subject to the previous fulfillment of military service obligations. Often Syrian dissenters abroad were granted documentation to return, merely in order to be arrested upon entering Syria. When Medhat Tayfour, for instance, who had left the country in 1983, applied for permission to return to Syria from Jordan, he was given a laissez-passer travel document but was arrested at the border on 1998 and never seen again. His brother was a member of the Muslim Brotherhood abroad. The strictly enforced rule of two-year military service for any Syrian abroad who did not complete it before emigrating (or pay a $15,000 waiver fee) is also a major factor prohibiting the return of Syrian youth. More recently, the proposed Law No. 10, or the "absentees law," of 2018 would allow the regime to confiscate land abandoned by those fleeing the Syrian civil war—a clear attempt at preventing those Syrians from returning home (Ibrahim 2018). More often than not, those who fled the country—including their spouses and children—are no longer able to obtain passports at Syrian embassies, which maintain 'black lists' of dissenters. When their existing passports expire, Syrians are effectively without documentation of Syrian nationality. As the Human Rights Watch reported:

> *Exiles also reported . . . that the names of children born to Syrian political exiles abroad could not be entered in Syria's civil status register, making it impossible for them to obtain passports and in effect depriving them of legal recognition of their Syrian nationality. The daughter of one exile, who left Syria with her mother and siblings when she was ten years old, said that her applications for a passport were repeatedly denied. Without a passport, she was unable to return to Syria to pursue advanced university studies and marry her Syrian fiancé. In another case, an exile reported that his son, who earned a medical degree in Jordan but lacked a passport, could not travel outside of Jordan for specialized medical studies. At a meeting in 1999 with nine Syrian women who were the wives or widows of political exiles, Human Rights Watch counted among them seventy-seven children without Syrian passports who were effectively stateless. The twenty-six-year-old daughter of one of the women said: "My father is dead. What is my crime? I have a right to my Syrian nationality and I want to go back to my country."* (Human Rights Watch n.d.)

**Egyptian emigrant policies.** While Egyptian migrants worked across the Arab world and Africa for most of the twentieth century (Awad and Selim 2017; Amin and Awni 1986), Egyptian migration increased significantly in the Sadat and Mubarak eras (1970–2011), toward both toward the oil-producing countries of the Arab world (Fergany 1983) and the West (Zohry and Harrell-Bond 2003). Sizable Egyptian migrant populations exist across the Arab world today, particularly in Saudi Arabia, as well as in Europe, North America, and Australia.

In contrast to the exit policies developed by Syria and Libya, post-1970 Egypt approached its citizens' emigration as a right (Dessouki 1982; Tsourapas 2015b). Article 52 of the 1971 Constitution declared that "Citizens shall now have the right to permanent or temporary migration" (Arab Republic of Egypt 1971). The Egyptian regime also introduced Presidential Decree 73/71, a law that would allow public-sector employees who emigrated in pursuit of employment abroad to be reinstated in their positions in Egypt, if they returned home within a year after their resignation, with any salary increments they missed to be taken into account (Ibrahim 1982:68). This right was expanded in the consolidated 1983 Migration Law—after 1983, migrants would be reinstated to their previous public-sector positions (or equivalent ones) if they returned within two years following their resignation. Egypt signed a number of agreements with Arab host states to facilitate labor migration (table 2). Egyptian school curricula were instructed to teach that "people emigrate, just like the birds" (*Al-Ahram al-Iqtisadi*, No. 745, 1983). In fact, the 1977 preparatory school certificate exam asked students to write an essay on "the joys of a person who could obtain work in an 'Arab' country" (*Al-Ahram*, May 18, 1977).

## Table 2. Emigration-related agreements between Egypt and other Arab states, 1971–2011
(treaties, memoranda of understanding, and protocols)

| Year | Countries |
| --- | --- |
| 1971 | Egypt–Libya |
| 1972 | Egypt–Algeria |
| 1974 | Egypt–Jordan<br>Egypt–Qatar |
| 1975 | Egypt–Iraq |
| 1981 | Egypt–Jordan |
| 1985 | Egypt–Jordan<br>Egypt–Iraq |
| 1993 | Egypt–Iraq<br>Egypt–Lebanon<br>Egypt–United Arab Emirates |
| 1994 | Egypt–United Arab Emirates<br>Egypt–Libya |
| 1997 | Egypt–Yemen |
| 1998 | Egypt–Lebanon |
| 2001 | Egypt–Tunisia |
| 2003 | Egypt–Sudan |
| 2007 | Egypt–Jordan<br>Egypt–Saudi Arabia |
| 2009 | Egypt–Libya |

Source: Tsourapas 2015b.

While individual cases of intimidation and monitoring do surface (MilanoToday 2017), the Egyptian diaspora policy has been generally characterized by a desire to reach out to these migrant and diaspora communities, primarily for developmental purposes (Tsourapas 2017). Not unlike other developing countries, a major aspect of Egypt's diaspora policy is built on the perceived political and economic gains of embracing its diaspora in the West. Despite a lack of precise statistical information on the matter, members of the Egyptian Coptic community (estimated at approximately 10% of the country's total population) were able to emigrate freely to North America, Europe, and Australia, with the Coptic diaspora now numbering between 1 and 2 million (Tadros 2013). Although most Copts settled permanently abroad, there were no obstacles in place to prevent their return. Similarly, their activities abroad were not subject to consistent monitoring or repression, allowing the Coptic diaspora to create vibrant, politically active communities, particularly in the US (Iskander 2012). Even at particularly tense moments between the Egyptian regime and its opposition members abroad in the early 1980s (see, for an overview, Heikal 1983), there has been little evidence of transnational repression.

A large number of Egyptian emigrants would frequently be invited back to Cairo and Alexandria, where they would be entertained by the President and the First Lady under the administrations of both presidents Sadat (*al-Gumhuriya*, August 4, 1976) and Mubarak (*Al-Ahram*, August 2, 2010). In the aftermath of the 1973 Arab–Israeli War, about 1,500 emigrants from North America would receive annual tours of the Suez war front hosted by various cabinet ministers (*Al-Ahram*, June 17, 1974; *al-Gumhuriya*, August 27, 1976). Those studying in Europe and North America would receive financial support from the Egyptian president on an ad hoc basis—a grant of $50,000, or approximately $212,000 today, was given to the Union of Egyptian Students in North America, for instance (*Al-Ahram*, August 9, 1976), while any problems were dealt with immediately, regardless of cost. At one point, Sadat even had the presidential airplane transport home Egyptians who had been unable to find employment in France (*al-Gumhuriya*, July 12, 1975). A number of different committees and other institutions developed that were responsible for Egyptians abroad, including a separate Ministry of State for Emigration Affairs (created in 1981), which was replaced in 1996 by the Ministry of Manpower and Emigration. In fact, Egyptian reliance on migrant labor has often been exploited by numerous host states, including Libya and Jordan, for their own political gains (Tsourapas 2018b).

Through the state's return policy, Egypt sought to have diaspora members contribute to the development of the homeland. The theme of citizens' return to the homeland, in particular, demonstrated that labor emigration was viewed not as an act of political treason, but as a necessity for Egypt's economic development. Mechanisms for the granting of dual citizenship to Egyptians were duly instituted. Egypt offered financial incentives (for instance, prioritized access to housing), and the ad hoc creation of "visiting professor" posts in universities to be occupied by Egyptian scientists residing abroad (*Al-Ahram*, April 21, 1974). Those who had emigrated illegally before 1970 (either as an act of political dissent or to escape the military draft) were free to return without prosecution: as Ali E. Hillal Dessouki, former minister of youth (1999–2004), recalled, President Sadat decided to grant a general amnesty to all Egyptians who had escaped conscription and dispatched military delegations abroad to settle questions of conscription and to invite the emigrants back to Egypt (personal interview, Cairo, April 13, 2014). More prominently, the acts of emigration and, importantly, return migration were approached as a matter of patriotism.

> *The skills of Egypt's youth have stolen the limelight and come to be the country's staple crop. Some of them get higher salaries than Dr. Henry Kissinger while still in their forties. Some lead the same lavish life as Hollywood stars. They own villas with fragrant gardens and as many as three cars each. One of them travels by private helicopter from his country home to his place of work in New York! But our country will not lose the brains we export to the outside world. For a successful Egyptian must be back home one day to drink again from the Nile and to live with the generous people [of Egypt]. An Egyptian travels but does not go for good, for he always returns.* (*al-Akhbar*, June 30, 1975)

**Turkish emigrant policies.** Turkey encouraged labor emigration from the late 1950s onward, primarily to Germany and, to a lesser extent, other Western countries (Sayari 1986). While Germany has remained a major destination ever since, Turkey also promoted labor emigration to the Arab world and Russia in the post-1973 era, as demand for immigrant labor in Europe declined.

As in Egypt, the Turkish authorities initially framed the state's exit policy in terms of the potential contribution of migration to the development of the Turkish state, economic and otherwise (Martin 1991). According to a 1964 report, labor migration would serve five aims, namely: helping the integration of the country into the European political and economic community; reducing underemployment as much as possible; increasing hard-currency revenues; providing knowledge, ability, and experience to unskilled and semi-skilled workers; and, by increasing the number of people with experience of European work methods, encouraging industries of the receiving countries to set up subsidiaries in Turkey.

As early as 1950, Turkish law stated that no exit visa was required to leave Turkey (Art. 7, Law No. 5682), and placed no restrictions on those already employed within Turkey: a 1975 SOPEMI report found that 81% of Turkish emigrants were already employed prior to emigration. In fact, as per its 1961 agreement with the Federal Republic of Germany, a liaison office was established in Istanbul that formed a branch of the German Bundesanstalt für Arbeit, which coordinated the recruitment process and made the final selection of emigrants on behalf of Germany.

Realizing the economic benefits of migrant remittances, Turkey engaged in a series of migration-related agreements with host states. When the 1973 oil embargo diminished Western Europe's appetite for immigrant labor, Turkish authorities targeted Libya, Jordan, and the oil-producing countries of the Gulf. Turkish policy did not discriminate against minorities, which enabled the emigration of thousands of Turkish Kurds, particularly in the post-1980 period. They have created a politically vibrant community abroad. As in Egypt, different ministries shared responsibility for these policies, including the ministries of Labour, Finance, Education, Foreign Affairs, Customs, and Local Affairs, as well as the Turkish Employment Service and the Turkish State Planning Organization.

At times of conflict with its Kurdish minority, the Turkish state did not place obstacles to emigration, particularly given that it does not recognize the existence of any minority groups within its borders. The first major influx of Kurds into Germany occurred following the 1961 bilateral agreement. The Kurdish Separatist Movement (PKK) was then able to mobilize from its base in Germany, particularly from the 1980s onward. Although the statistics are not precise, estimates place the Kurdish diaspora in Europe at roughly 850,000, of whom more than half a million reside in Germany. Like the Egyptian Coptic diaspora, and unlike the cases of Libya and Syria, the Kurdish diaspora has an extensive history of political mobilization.

With regard to its diaspora policy, Turkey developed extensive outreach mechanisms for its diaspora populations, particularly within Europe (Østergaard-Nielsen 2003). These evolved out of the need to organize the dispatch of economic remittances into a broader set of policies that provided social assistance and support of diasporic organizations abroad. Dedicated institutions—such as the Office for Turks Abroad and Related Communities (YTB)—have been created with an economic, sociocultural, but also political rationale. Turkey seeks to ensure the well-being of its communities abroad, but also, by projecting 'soft power' through these communities, to have a greater say in EU states' politics.

Finally, the state's return policy involves a number of provisions put in place for returnees. Turkish law states that no visa is needed (Art. 5, Law No. 5682). Article 23 of the Constitution also states that no citizen may be deprived of the right to return to the homeland. Yet it is important to note that, unlike Egypt, Turkish diaspora policy has not prioritized the issue of emigrants' return, primarily due to its perceived economic cost.

**Jordanian emigrant policies.** Jordan encouraged labor emigration from the late 1950s onward, and maintains an open-door policy that does not require exit permits or other special permissions, similar to Egypt (Brand 2006; Shami 1999). The majority of Jordanian emigration flows toward the Arab oil-producing countries of the Gulf—by the 1970s, around 60% of the Jordanian labor force was working in the Gulf (Thiollet 2011). These flows have continued until today, with the exception of a period of economic downturn and return migration from the mid 1980s to the early 2000s.

Jordan has facilitated emigration through its exit policy. This has included a number of bilateral agreements with host states, starting with a Jordanian–Kuwaiti accord in 1958, followed by agreements with Pakistan and Libya in 1978. Together with Egypt and (pre-Assad) Syria, Jordan also signed a 1967 agreement calling for the free circulation of workers in the Arab world. Jordan has ceased keeping detailed records of emigration flows, much as Egypt has done, ostensibly as part of abolishing any controls or monitoring of cross-border mobility. Within policy circles, labor emigration was viewed not as a political act, but as one that would positively contribute to the country's economic development. The government abolished exit permit requirements in 1962, as the state gradually realized the economic importance of preserving emigration flows, particularly to the Arab oil-producing states.

Importantly, in the period under examination, Jordan did not discriminate in its exit policy between Jordanians and Palestinian citizens. While relations between the ruling Hashemite monarchy and the Palestinian leadership became quite tense, particularly with regard to the policies developed by Yasser Arafat and the PLO in the 1970s, the regime did not use its exit policy as an instrument of control over the Palestinian community. At the same time, Brand's research highlights how Jordan has attempted to normalize the phenomenon of labor migration through its treatment in textbooks, another aspect that is reminiscent of Egypt's permissive exit policies. The 2010 Jordanian tenth-grade civics textbook, for instance, highlights how countries such as Egypt and Jordan benefited from migration to the Gulf, and states that "with the tremendous flow of oil in the Gulf region and in Libya, new waves of population and labor force movement began, employment opportunities expanded . . . and the processes of migration and movement of labor to the oil regions became one of the more important forces shaping contemporary Arab life" (Brand 2010:105).

Jordan's diaspora policy was similarly permissive. The Ministry of Foreign Affairs established a special section on expatriate affairs in 1981. The 1981–1985 Five-Year Plan laid out specific strategies for the dispatch of labor attachés to the main destination countries, such as Kuwait and the United Arab Emirates, in order to resolve any problems and support expatriates' activities. In 1987, Jordan decided to establish an Expatriates Directorate (*mudiriyat al-mughtaribin*) in the Ministry of Labor and Social Development. It also initiated a series of expatriate conferences, which would annually invite hundreds of Jordanians residing abroad back to the homeland in order to share their opinions on how to further develop linkages with the diaspora. Although these conferences were cut short following the tumultuous Arab–Israeli politics of the post-Intifada era, they attest to the state's desires to develop links with its communities abroad. As King Husayn stated in his speech delivered during the First Expatriate Conference: "Our country lacks natural resources, but its richness stems from its people, who are highly educated and have proved themselves to be the best technicians, professionals, businessmen, and intellectuals, whether inside or outside Jordan" (*Jordan Times*, July 21, 1985).

Finally, Jordan's policy of return was also approached in a permissive manner. By 1987, the Jordanian Parliament had responded to expatriate requests and approved dual citizenship (*Jordan Times*, July 18, 1987). Those who participated in the Expatriate Conferences were taken on tours of development projects across Jordan and were told about state initiatives that would allow them to pursue economic activities back in the homeland. They were offered special hotel rates (according to instructions by the Ministry of Tourism and Antiquities) and flight tickets on Royal Jordanian Airlines (cf. *Jordan Times*, July 14, 1986). At the same time, a number of investment initiatives have been launched since the early 1970s. These include the Encouragement of Investment Law No. 53/1972 with respect to the 1973 Post Office Fund; the development of specific bonds in 1974 designed to encourage investment of remittances within Jordan; and more recent initiatives, such as the 1995 Investment Promotion Law (Brand 2006:210).

## Conclusion

This chapter has attempted to fill a gap in the existing literature on state–diaspora relations by examining how authoritarian emigration states, in particular, develop multi-tier policies that target population groups at various stages in their mobility. By arguing that non-democracies have the capacity to generate, shape, and dismantle diasporas, I demonstrate how diaspora engagement policies need to be broken down into *exit*, *diaspora*, and *return* policies, respectively. Beyond shifting the focus of the state–diaspora relations literature on the global South, I also provide a coherent argument against treating such policies as unitary. All five of the Middle Eastern countries examined (Libya, Syria, Egypt, Turkey, and

Jordan) have developed complex policies that targeted populations differently at different times—before, during, and after their time spent abroad.

How applicable is my argumentation beyond the five cases examined here? A cursory examination suggests that similar patterns appear in other illiberal contexts. A number of Middle Eastern states have developed similar, multi-tier diaspora policies: Tunisia and Morocco, for instance, developed exit and return policies that encouraged labor emigration to Western Europe in a permissive manner, similar to the policies developed by Egypt, Turkey, and Jordan. At the same time, both states developed diaspora policies that involved intense surveillance of their diaspora groups abroad, reminiscent of Libyan and Syrian strategies (Brand 2002). The October 2018 murder of journalist Jamal Khashoggi inside the Saudi Arabian consulate in Istanbul constitutes a more recent, clear case of Saudi Arabia's repressive policy toward its political dissenters in the diaspora. Beyond the Middle East, autocratic or illiberal regimes approach state–diaspora relations in similar multi-tier strategies. In June 2017, Vietnam denationalized political dissident Pham Minh Hoang, a member of the Vietnam Reform Party that the government considers a 'terrorist group,' preventing his return to the homeland ("Vietnam Exiles Dissident" 2017). Under the Soviet Union, the emigration of minority groups—particularly Jews—was closely monitored in a manner similar to Libyan or Syrian exit policies (Peretz 2015).

Beyond establishing the different diaspora policy tiers that Middle East states have developed, further work is necessary in order to understand policy variation, both across time and over cases. A key question emerges from the comparison: why do Libya and Syria appear to have developed more repressive policies than Egypt, Turkey, or Jordan? Perhaps this relates to the degree of domestic repression or, put differently, the extent to which political and security priorities overshadow economic or developmental goals. A tentative explanation might be that, given their material reliance on emigration and migrant remittances, Egyptian, Turkish, and Jordanian elites are less prone to engage in transnational repression than their Libyan and Syrian counterparts. Within-case variation also needs to be further substantiated. In the brief post–Arab Spring processes of political liberalization, Egypt and Libya shifted toward more permissive diaspora policies by introducing out-of-country voting processes; the Syrian regime allowed the return of exiled dissidents in 2000, when Bashar al-Assad took power after his father's death, instituting the so-called Damascus Spring. On the other hand, autocracies' shift toward repression also affects their diaspora policies: since mid 2016, Erdoğan has adopted an increasingly repressive exit policy, most recently banning the emigration of any academics and ordering those abroad to return immediately. The varied means through which autocracies and illiberal democracies construct multi-tier diaspora policies constitute an unexplored dimension of the state–diaspora relations literature.

## References

Adamson, Fiona. 2016. "The Growing Importance of Diaspora Politics," *Current History*, 115(784): 291–297.

———. 2019. "Sending States and the Making of Intra-Diasporic Politics: Turkey and Its Diaspora(s)," *International Migration Review*. https://doi.org/10.1177/0197918318767665

Alemán, José, and Dwayne Woods. 2014. "No Way Out: Travel Restrictions and Authoritarian Regimes," *Migration and Development*, 3(2): 285–305.

Amin, Galal A., and Elizabeth Taylor Awni. 1986. *Hijrat al-'amala al-Misriya: dirasa naqdiya li-l-buhuth wa-l-dirasat al-khassa bi-hijrat al-'amala al-Misriya ila al-kharij*. Ottawa: Markaz al-Buhuth li-l-Tanmiya al-Dawliyah.

Arab Republic of Egypt. 1971. Constitution. Cairo: Arab Republic of Egypt.

Awad, Ibrahim, and Hedayat Selim. 2017. "Labour Migration Governance in Times of Political Transition: A Comparative Analysis of Egypt and Tunisia," *Migration and Development*, 6(1): 1–13.

Blatter, Joachim. 2011. "Dual Citizenship and Theories of Democracy," *Citizenship Studies*, 15(6–7): 769–798.

Brand, Laurie A. 2002. "States and Their Expatriates: Explaining the Development of Tunisian and Moroccan Emigration-Related Institutions." University of California–San Diego. Working Paper No. 52. La Jolla, CA: University of Southern California.

———. 2006. *Citizens Abroad: Emigration and the State in the Middle East and North Africa*. Cambridge: Cambridge University Press.

———. 2010. "National Narratives and Migration: Discursive Strategies of Inclusion and Exclusion in Jordan and Lebanon," *International Migration Review*, 44(1): 78–110.
———. 2014. "Arab Uprisings and the Changing Frontiers of Transnational Citizenship: Voting from Abroad in Political Transitions," *Political Geography*, 41(July): 54–63.
Bredeloup, Sylvie, and Olivier Pliez. 2011. "The Libyan Migration Corridor." Research Report. Florence: Migration Policy Institute.
Brinkerhoff, Jennifer M., ed. 2008. *Diasporas and Development: Exploring the Potential*. Boulder: Lynne Rienner Publishers.
Caramani, Daniele, and Florian Grotz. 2015. "Beyond Citizenship and Residence? Exploring the Extension of Voting Rights in the Age of Globalization," *Democratization*, 22(5): 799–819.
Chalcraft, John. 2008. *The Invisible Cage: Syrian Migrant Workers in Lebanon*. Stanford, CA: Stanford University Press.
Collyer, Michael, ed. 2013. *Emigration Nations: Policies and Ideologies of Emigrant Engagement*. New York: Palgrave Macmillan.
Cooley, Alexander A., and John Heathershaw. 2017. *Dictators without Borders: Power and Money in Central Asia*. New Haven, CT: Yale University Press.
De Haas, Hein. 2007. "North-African Migration Systems: Evolution, Transformations and Development Linkages," *International Migration Institute*, 6: 5–6.
Délano, Alexandra. 2011. *Mexico and Its Diaspora in the United States: Policies of Emigration since 1848*. New York: Cambridge University Press.
———. 2014. "The Diffusion of Diaspora Engagement Policies: A Latin American Agenda," *Political Geography*, 41 (July): 90–100.
Dessouki, Ali E. Hillal. 1982. "The Shift in Egypt's Migration Policy: 1952–1978," *Middle Eastern Studies*, 18(1): 53–68.
Escribà-Folch, Abel, Covadonga Meseguer, and Joseph Wright. 2015. "Remittances and Democratization," *International Studies Quarterly*, 59(3): 571–586.
Fergany, Nader. 1983. *Al-Hijra ila al-naft: ab'ad al-hijra li-l-'amal fi-l-buldan al-naftiya wa atharuha 'ala al-tanmiya fi-l-watan al-'arabi*. Beirut: Markaz Dirasat al-Wahda al-'Arabiya.
Fitzgerald, David. 2009. *A Nation of Emigrants: How Mexico Manages Its Migration*. Berkeley: University of California Press.

Gamlen, Alan. 2008. "The Emigration State and the Modern Geopolitical Imagination," *Political Geography*, 27(8): 840–856.

———. 2014. "Diaspora Institutions and Diaspora Governance." *International Migration Review*, 48 (September): S180–217.

Glasius, Marlies. 2017. "Extraterritorial Authoritarian Practices: A Framework," *Globalizations*, 15(2): 179–197.

Greenhill, Kelly M. 2010. *Weapons of Mass Migration: Forced Displacement, Coercion, and Foreign Policy*. Ithaca, NY: Cornell University Press.

Guevarra, Anna Romina. 2009. *Marketing Dreams, Manufacturing Heroes: The Transnational Labor Brokering of Filipino Workers*. New Brunswick, NJ: Rutgers University Press.

Gumrukcu, Tuvan. 2017. "Erdogan Says Referendum Turnout among Turks Abroad Jumps." Reuters, April 12. https://www.reuters.com/article/us-turkey-referendum-expats/erdogan-says-referendum-turnout-among-turks-abroad-jumps-idUSKBN17D29B

Heikal, Mohamed Hassanein. 1983. *Autumn of Fury: The Assassination of Anwar Sadat*. London: Andre Deutch.

Hirt, Nicole, and Abdulkader Saleh Mohammad. 2017. "By Way of Patriotism, Coercion, or Instrumentalization: How the Eritrean Regime Makes Use of the Diaspora to Stabilize Its Rule," *Globalizations*, 15(2): 232–247.

Hollifield, James F. 2004. "The Emerging Migration State," *International Migration Review*, 38(3): 885–912.

Human Rights Watch. n.d. "Syria—Human Rights Developments." https://www.hrw.org/legacy/wr2k/Mena-09.htm.

Ibrahim, Arwa. 2018. "Syria: 'Absentees Law' Could See Millions of Refugees Lose Lands." April 7. https://www.aljazeera.com/news/2018/04/syria-absentees-law-millions-refugees-lose-lands-180407073139495.html

Ibrahim, Saad Eddin. 1982. *The New Arab Social Order; A Study on the Social Impact of Oil Wealth*. Boulder: Westview.

Iskander, Elizabeth. 2012. *Sectarian Conflict in Egypt: Coptic Media, Identity, and Representation*. New York: Routledge.

Iskander, Natasha. 2010. *Creative State: Forty Years of Migration and Development Policy in Morocco and Mexico*. Ithaca, NY: Cornell University Press.

King, Charles, and Neil J. Melvin. 2006. "Diaspora Politics: Ethnic Linkages, Foreign Policy, and Security in Eurasia," *International Security*, 24(3): 108–138.
Koinova, Maria. 2017. "Why Erdoğan Is Chasing Turkey's Overseas Voters So Hard." The Conversation. http://theconversation.com/why-erdogan-is-chasing-turkeys-overseas-voters-so-hard-74469
———. 2018. "Sending States and Diaspora Positionality in International Relations," *International Political Sociology*, 12(2): 190–210.
Koinova, Maria, and Gerasimos Tsourapas. 2018. "How Do Countries of Origin Engage Migrants and Diasporas? Multiple Actors and Comparative Perspectives," *International Political Science Review*, 39(3): 311–321.
Leblang, David. 2011. "Harnessing the Diaspora: Dual Citizenship, Migrant Remittances and Return," *Comparative Political Studies*, 50(1): 75–101.
Margheritis, Ana. 2015. *Migration Governance across Regions: State–Diaspora Relations in the Latin America–Southern Europe Corridor*. New York: Taylor & Francis Limited.
Markowitz, Fran, and Anders H. Stefansson, eds. 2004. "Homecomings to the Future: From Diasporic Mythographies to Social Projects of Return." In Fran Markowitz and Anders H. Stefansson, eds. *Homecomings: Unsettling Paths of Return*, 2–20. Lanham: Lexington Books.
Martin, Philip L. 1991. *The Unfinished Story: Turkish Labour Migration to Western Europe with Special Reference to the Federal Republic of Germany*. Geneva: International Labour Office.
MilanoToday. 2017. "Donne E Uomini Picchiati, Umiliati, Sequestrati E Minacciati Nel Consolato D'egitto a Milano." MilanoToday, April 19. http://www.milanotoday.it/cronaca/picchiati-consolato-egiziano.html
Mirilovic, Nikola. 2014. "Regime Type, International Migration, and the Politics of Dual Citizenship Toleration," *International Political Science Review*, 36(5), 510–525.
Moss, Dana M. 2016. "Transnational Repression, Diaspora Mobilization, and the Case of the Arab Spring," *Social Problems*, 63(4): 480–498.
Mylonas, Harris. 2013. "Ethnic Return Migration, Selective Incentives, and the Right to Freedom of Movement in Post–Cold War Greece." In Willem Maas, ed. *Democratic Citizenship and the Free Movement of People*, 175–193. Leiden: Martinus Nijhoff Publishers.

Natter, Katharina. 2015. "Revolution and Political Transition in Tunisia: A Migration Game Changer?" Washington, DC: Migration Policy Institute.

Naujoks, Daniel. 2013. *Migration, Citizenship, and Development: Diasporic Membership Policies and Overseas Indians in the United States.* New Delhi: Oxford University Press.

Østergaard-Nielsen, Eva. 2003. "Turkey and the 'Euro Turks': Overseas Nationals as an Ambiguous Asset." In E. Østergaard-Nielsen, ed., *International Migration and Sending Countries: Perceptions, Policies and Transnational Relations*, 77–98. Houndmills: Palgrave Macmillan.

Paoletti, Emanuela. 2011. "Migration and Foreign Policy: The Case of Libya," *The Journal of North African Studies*, 16(2): 215–231.

Pargeter, Alison. 2012. *Libya: The Rise and Fall of Qaddafi.* New Haven, CT: Yale University Press.

Parolin, Gianluca Paolo. 2009. *Citizenship in the Arab World: Kin, Religion and Nation-State.* Amsterdam: Amsterdam University Press.

Peretz, Pauline. 2015. *Let My People Go: The Transnational Politics of Soviet Jewish Emigration during the Cold War.* Vol. 1. Piscataway, NJ: Transaction Publishers.

Philipp, Thomas. 1985. *The Syrians in Egypt: 1725–1975.* Vol. 3. London: Coronet Books.

Rodriguez, Robyn Magalit. 2010. *Migrants for Export: How the Philippine State Brokers Labor to the World.* Minneapolis: University of Minnesota Press.

Sayari, S. 1986. "Migration Policies of Sending Countries: Perspectives on the Turkish Experience," *The Annals of the American Academy of Political and Social Science*, 485: 87–97.

Shain, Yossi. 2005. *The Frontier of Loyalty: Political Exiles in the Age of the Nation-State.* Ann Arbor: University of Michigan Press.

Shami, Seteney. 1999. "Emigration Dynamics in Jordan, Palestine and Lebanon." In R. Appleyard, ed. *Emigration Dynamics in Developing Countries*, 128–201. Aldershot: Ashgate.

Smart, Alan, and Jinn-Yuh Hsu. 2004. "The Chinese Diaspora, Foreign Investment and Economic Development in China," *The Review of International Affairs*, 3(4): 544–566.

# References

Tadros, Mariz. 2013. *Copts at the Crossroads: The Challenges of Building Inclusive Democracy in Contemporary Egypt*. Cairo: American University in Cairo Press.

Thiollet, Hélène. 2011. "Migration as Diplomacy: Labor Migrants, Refugees, and Arab Regional Politics in the Oil-Rich Countries," *International Labor and Working-Class History*, 79(1): 103–121.

"To Silence Dissidents, Gulf States Are Revoking Their Citizenship." 2016. *The Economist*, November 26. http://www.economist.com/news/middle-east-and-africa/21710679-many-are-left-stateless-result-silence-dissidents-gulf-states-are

Tsourapas, Gerasimos. 2015a. "The Politics of Egyptian Migration to Libya." Middle East Research and Information Project. http://www.merip.org/mero/mero031715

———. 2015b. "Why Do States Develop Multi-Tier Emigrant Policies? Evidence from Egypt," *Journal of Ethnic and Migration Studies*, 41(13): 2192–2214.

———. 2016. "Nasser's Educators and Agitators across *al-Watan al-'Arabi*: Tracing the Foreign Policy Importance of Egyptian Regional Migration, 1952–1967," *British Journal of Middle Eastern Studies*, 43(3): 324–341.

———. 2017. "Migration Diplomacy in the Global South: Cooperation, Coercion and Issue-Linkage in Gaddafi's Libya," *Third World Quarterly*, 38(10): 2367–2385.

———. 2018a. "Authoritarian Emigration States: Soft Power and Cross-Border Mobility in the Middle East," *International Political Science Review*, 39(3): 400–416.

———. 2018b. "Labor Migrants as Political Leverage: Migration Interdependence and Coercion in the Mediterranean," *International Studies Quarterly*, 62(2): 383–395.

———. 2018c. "Theorizing State-Diaspora Relations in the Middle East: Authoritarian Emigration States in Comparative Perspective," *Mediterranean Politics*, DOI: 10.1080/13629395.2018.1511299.

US Department of State. 1994. "1993 Human Rights Report: Libya." http://dosfan.lib.uic.edu/ERC/democracy/1993_hrp_report/93hrp_report_nea/Libya.html.

Vandewalle, Dirk. 2012. *A History of Modern Libya*. 2nd ed. Cambridge: Cambridge University Press.

Varadarajan, Latha. 2010. *The Domestic Abroad: Diasporas in International Relations*. New York: Oxford University Press.
"Vietnam Exiles Dissident after Revoking His Citizenship." 2017. Al-Jazeera, June 26. http://www.aljazeera.com/news/2017/06/vietnam-exiles-dissident-revoking-citizenship-170625150005282.html
Winckler, Onn. 1997. "Syrian Migration to the Arab Oil-Producing Countries," *Middle Eastern Studies*, 33(1): 107–118.
World Bank. 2011. *Migration and Remittances Handbook*. Washington, DC: World Bank.
Zohry, Ayman, and Barbara Harrell-Bond. 2003. *Contemporary Egyptian Migration: An Overview of Voluntary and Forced Migration*. Sussex: Development Research Centre on Migration, Globalisation and Poverty.

CHAPTER 7

# Interest Groups and Refugee Policy Making: The Case of Germany

*Maysa Ayoub*

## Introduction

Following the influx of Syrians and other refugees to Europe and the inability of the EU to address the issue collectively, European states started unilaterally to close their borders one after the other.[1] Until 2016, Germany was the only state left among the 28 EU member states that kept its borders open. It was only in March 2017 that the German parliament adopted stricter asylum measures, known as Asylum Package II (Mayer 2016:1).

In an attempt to understand the reason behind Germany's open-door policy, this chapter focuses on the influence of interest groups on policy making. It adopts the theoretical orientation of the "Social Construction of the Targeted Population" theory and assumes that the political power of refugees (the target population) could be measured by the number and type of interest groups working on their behalf. Thus, the chapter will analyze the activities of interest groups in Germany and examine their influence on the German government's response to the refugee crisis, from the initial open-door policy to the recent stricter asylum legislation.

## Interest Groups

Interest groups are defined by some scholars on the basis of behavior and by others on the basis of organizational structure. For the former,

---

1 The author would like to thank Ms. Karima Abdel Aziz, research assistant and graduate of the University of Siegen, who gathered the information on interest groups in Germany and assisted in the writing of this chapter.

an interest group is any group whose activities are for the purpose of influencing policy outcomes, thus including a wider array of social movements. The latter, on the other hand, provides a narrower definition, including as interest groups only those that have an organizational structure. Another distinction is often made, regarding the nature of the interest being represented by the group. There are groups that represent the narrow economic interest of their members—examples include trade unions, business groups, and professional organizations—and there are groups that work for a broad public cause. Finally, there are scholars who classify interest groups according to the scope of their activities, distinguishing between general interest groups and those that specialize in a limited number of issues (Baroni, Brendan, Chalmers, Luz, and Rasmussen 2014:141–143).

Interest groups concerned with migration and refugee issues fall under the category of public interest groups working for a broader public cause. In Germany, they are divided into two categories of organizations/movements: rights-based human rights organizations that are working on promoting refugee rights, and right-wing anti-migrant movements. In addition, refugees and migrants organize themselves into groups, known as Home Town Associations, to promote their own interests.

Social constructionism holds that social problems are not neutral or objective phenomena; rather, social problems are an interpretation of conditions that are subjectively defined as problematic. Thus the formulation of policies toward a particular social issue would to a great extent depend on how the issue is perceived and labeled. This chapter adopts the concept of the "Social Construction of the Targeted Population," as developed by Helen Ingram and Anne Schneider. According to this concept, policies have target populations, and the extent to which policy design would benefit or burden the target population of the policy depends upon two factors: the political power of the target population and their positive or negative social constructions (Ingram, Schneider, and DeLeon 2007:96–101).

This chapter analyzes the political power of refugees (the target population) by analyzing the number and type of interest groups working on their behalf and their ability to develop a positive construct of them. How many liberal pro-migrants' rights groups operate in Germany as compared to right-wing anti-migrant groups? Which type is able to rally public support and/or is connected to policy makers? How is the target population constructed in the mind of each kind of interest group? The chapter will try to answer these and other questions to explain the policy adopted by Germany in the face of the Syrian refugee crisis.

The next section will discuss the importance of interest groups in Germany in general and their involvement in the policy process. This will be followed by an explanation of the organizational structure and resources of the three different types of refugee interest groups in Germany and how each group perceives and labels 'refugees.'

**Interest groups in Germany.** Article 9 of Germany's Basic Law (the German constitution) stresses freedom of association as a constitutional right and emphasizes that interest groups should be engaged in the political process. Moreover, the rules of procedure of the Bundestag (the German Parliament) and the federal government encourage interest groups' contributions to the policy process (Geoffrey 2009:167–169).

Interest groups attempt to influence policy by influencing public opinion and by direct communication with political parties, the legislature, and the executive. Political parties are usually associated with or sympathetic to particular interests, and some parties invite interest groups as expert advisers during the discussion of a policy. Interest groups campaign to bring members of the party associated with their interests to power (Geoffrey 2009:167–169). With regard to their connection to the legislature, a member of an interest group could be a member of parliament. If a policy affects that interest group, the member who is associated with the group will try to exert influence either to promote or to discourage the policy. This strategy is referred to as 'internal lobbying,' which describes a situation where the demands of the interest group are represented directly in the parliament (Flentje 2015:11). Finally, the connection between the government and an interest group could be either indirect, through political parties, or direct, in the form of a delegation to the relevant ministry. Interest groups are able to exert influence on the government because the rules of procedures of the federal government allow for consultation with interest groups during the process of preparing legislation (Geoffrey 2009:167–169).

The influence of interest groups on the legislature and executive can be exerted through both direct and indirect lobbying strategies. Direct lobbying strategies include disseminating research results and technical information to policy makers and engaging in drafting legislation. Indirect lobbying, on the other hand, includes running the campaigns of political parties and raising public awareness to mobilize the public. 'Running campaigns' refers to attempts to influence elections in order to help elect or reelect candidates who support the interest groups' views (Macedo de Jesus 2010:70–74).

The success of both the direct and indirect strategies depends on three factors: the political structure, the characterization of the issue, and the resources of the interest groups. The resources of the interest group include financial as well as non-financial resources, such as the number of members and the size of staff. With regard to the political structure, the more accountable and democratic the political system, the higher the likelihood that it will take into consideration the opinion of organized groups. The less accountable the political system, the less likelihood that political institutions will take society's voice into account. The characterization of the issue refers to the nature of the issue the interest group is advocating for. According to previous research, interest groups are less likely to be successful in advocating for an issue that has far-reaching policy implications, is controversial, or has a high level of public awareness (noticeable issue). The reason for this is that controversial issues with major policy implications create different points of view that make it difficult for policy makers to make a decision. Moreover, when an issue has a high level of public awareness, policy makers are usually cautious in following the recommendations of interest groups (Macedo de Jesus 2010:70–74).

Germany is a democratically open country and has a history of encouraging participation in the policy process. The asylum issue, however, is a controversial one, with a high level of public awareness and far-reaching policy implications. The next section will discuss the third factor, which is the organizational structure and resources of each kind of refugees' interest group.

**Refugee rights organizations.** There are many rights-based organizations in Germany working for the cause of refugees' protection. The majority among them have sustainable financial resources and large numbers of members. For example, Pro Asyl, the largest German pro-immigration advocacy organization, has 21,000 members who contribute to its financial resources (Pro Asyl 2014/2015).

Pro Asyl and five other German organizations are members of the European Council on Refugees and Exiles (ECRE). The ECRE is a pan-European alliance of 90 NGOs protecting and advancing the rights of refugees, asylum seekers, and displaced persons. The mission of the ECRE is to promote the establishment of fair and humane European asylum policies and practices in accordance with international human rights law (ECRE website).

All five of the German organizations in the ECRE, including those whose mandate is humanitarian and not advocacy, are engaged in debate on policies concerning refugees. For example, Paritätische, Germany's largest umbrella organization of self-help initiatives in the area of health and social work, describes itself on its website as an organization that "represents its member organizations vis-à-vis government authorities and gives them a strong voice in the political arena" (Der Paritätische Gesamtverband website). Likewise, the stated mission of Caritas on its website is that it offers help and "represents [refugees'] interest in the world of politics and in the public sphere, and works towards a peaceful and open society" (Caritas Germany website).

**Xenophobic anti-migrant groups in Germany.** Following the Second World War, social and political movements aiming to revive the far-right wing, widely referred to as neo-Nazism, emerged in western Germany. The movement had very minimum popular support and was rarely able to organize any major activity. However, it started to gain momentum after the reunification of East and West Germany. The reunification brought economic and political changes to the people who were part of what was known as East Germany. Economically, they had never experienced working in a free market economy. Thus they were exposed for the first time to the impact of unemployment without social welfare provision. Politically, they had no experience of democracy or free elections. Moreover, under the communist regime, youth were engaged in many activities organized by the Freie Deutsche Jugend (Free German Youth), which was operated by the Sozialistische

Einheitspartei (Communist Union Party). With the reunification, these structures disappeared, leaving young people in a social vacuum, easily targeted by extremist groups. In 1992–1993, Turkish migrant families were attacked twice by these groups, leaving five people dead (Hoehl 1995). Following these incidents, penalties were imposed on any organization engaged in activities that promote racism or anti-migrant sentiments, giving the authorities the right to close it down and confisciate its property (German Criminal Code, Section 130).

As a result, in order to evade state authorities, extreme-right organizations organize their activities through a loose structure known as *Kameradschaften* (comradeships). Internally, however, these comradeships have a structure and a leadership. Many of them were able to connect with right-wing groups in other parts of Europe. For example, authorities in Germany were able to identify connections between the comradeships based in Dortmund and those based in Holland, Bulgaria, and the Czech Republic. The German authorities estimate their number to be around 150, spread all over the different German states (Martin 2012).

In 2014, a new anti-migrant movement emerged in response to Germany's open-door policy toward Syrian refugees. The movement, known as PEGIDA, an acronym for "Patriotische Europäer gegen die Islamisierung des Abendlandes" (Patriotic Europeans against the Islamization of the West) was established in the state of Saxony, where most of its supporters are. Its establishment encouraged the development of other movements in other parts of the country, for example, the Bogida movement in Bonn and similar movements in Munich, Berlin, and Düsseldorf (Hoeks 2016:6). Although PEGIDA has an organizational structure and is registered as a voluntary organization, it has very few formal members; these constitute its leadership and speak at its events. Its supporters mainly attend its protests and demonstrations but are not registered members. The number of its supporters is not known, but it is estimated that they range between 25,000 and 40,000 throughout Germany (Pro Asyl 2014:26). PEGIDA calls for protecting the Judeo-Christian western culture, advocates for strict migration and asylum policies and tougher deportation measures, is intolerant of crimes committed by migrants, and rejects what it describe as 'parallel societies' such as the sharia courts. Although the movement rejects the label of a far-right movement, neo-Nazis take part in its protest activities (Knight 2017).

In addition to PEGIDA, a number of so-called 'civil initiatives' have emerged in response to specific events in specific cities. For instance, the Bürgerinitiative Marzahn-Hellersdorf was founded specifically in order to protest against building a refugee shelter in Hellersdorf. This was followed by a number of other civil initiatives in other parts of Germany, including Schneeberg wehrt sich (Schneeberg Defends Itself), which mobilized protesters and organized demonstrations against a planned refugee shelter in the city. The initiative first emerged on social media. On November 1, 2013, 1,800 people gathered in a torchlight procession to demonstrate against the shelter. The shelter in Schneeberg at that time accommodated 500, people but by the end of November 2013, the number was reduced to 230. This was attributed to the voluntary departure of refugees, who did not want to live in a xenophobic environment (Pro Asyl 2014:4–5).

The so-called civil initiatives are often established anonymously online on social networks like Facebook, without stating a name, telephone number, address, or contact person. They agitate openly against refugees. Anonymous profiles are created that invite people to "spontaneous" actions and demonstrations against refugees. It is argued that these initiatives are often created by members of the National Democratic Party of Germany (NPD), an extreme right party, or by representatives of comradeships, who often act in the background of these initiatives. Facebook thus becomes a basic technique for distributing different right-wing images from pages advocating an apparent "civil" image to other pages that openly discriminate against refugees (Pro Asyl 2014:11). Social media offer great potential for mobilizing and recruiting new members into neo-Nazi groups, allowing people to express their xenophobic, socially unacceptable beliefs more radically and freely (Pro Asyl 2014:23). Furthermore, nationwide alliances can be built more easily online than in real life. The names of Facebook pages show strong connections among the various initiatives. Most of them are given names such as "Nein zum Heim" ("No to the Shelter"), "X wehrt sich" ("X Defends Itself"), or "Asylflut stoppen" ("Stopping the Asylum Flood"). These pages often employ links to other websites representing similar ideological views. The protective anonymity that

Facebook offers allows this propaganda to be spread by apparently non-right-wing civilians under fake profiles, which makes it easier for the broad public to align themselves with these thoughts without aligning themselves strictly and openly with the NPD ideology. The internet thus provides a civil mask for a socially unacceptable ideology, making it easier to propagate (Pro Asyl 2014:26–27).

**Home Town Associations.** Home Town Associations (HTAs) are associations formed by immigrants from the same region of origin. The literature suggests that they have two main functions; one relates to the country of origin and the second relates to the country of destination. The function in relation to the destination country is to develop a sense of community while adjusting to their new life, offer support to newcomers, and maintain their culture and heritage through social activities. The function in relation to the country of origin is to support economic and political development in their countries of origin. Most of the academic literature focuses on the second function, the relation between HTAs and economic development in the countries of origin. Few studies have examined the impact of HTA activities on the receiving countries, and there is a lively debate between those who believe that HTAs foster migrants' integration and those who believe that they hinder integration and promote isolation (Orozco and Garcia-Zanello 2009:57). In the case of Germany, the vast majority of immigrants are Turkish, but it is also home to many immigrants from eastern and southern Europe as well as Africa and the Middle East (Eurostat).

A recent report by the Maastricht Graduate School of Governance mapped Syrian HTAs in Germany, discussing their work as well as the number and composition of their members. The report indicates that Syrian organizations existed in Germany long before the Syrian conflict of 2011, as Syrian migration to Germany dates back to the 1980s. However, the number of these organizations has increased significantly since 2011. Syrian HTAs, like other HTAs in Germany, depend on membership fees and donations. From its study of 60 Syrian HTAs throughout Germany, the report suggests that Syrian HTAs can be divided into five categories based on their activities. The first category consists of those that focus on activities that promote the integration of Syrian refugees in Germany. The vast majority of HTAs fall within this category. The second and third categories also include a large number of oganizations. The second category focuses on the provision of humanitarian aid to Syrians in Syria as well as to Syrians in neighboring countries, and the third category seeks to engage in sustainable development initiatives in Syria. The fourth category includes only a few organizations and focuses on activities that promote civil society development in Syria. The fifth and last category includes very few organizations (less than 15% of all Syrian HTAs in Germany), and consists of organizations that are active in the cultural area, focusing on promoting community building within the Syrian diaspora (Siegel, Ragab, and Rahmeier 2017:25–45).

## The Syrian Refugee Crisis

In September 2013, the number of Syrian refugees reached two million, putting immense pressures on the neighboring countries that are hosting them. Moreover, an increased trend was documented of refugees attempting to reach Europe irregularly. Responding to the crisis, the United Nations High Commissioner for Refugees (UNHCR), in its 2013 Syria Regional Response Plan, asked developed countries to offer 10,000 places to Syrians for humanitarian admission and 2,000 for resettlement (European Resettlement Network). This section will present the number of Syrians admitted to Germany through the German borders and through resettlement, explain Germany's asylum regulations, and review the amendments recently introduced to asylum regulations.

**Claiming asylum (through regular or irregular travel).** Direct asylum claims in Europe by citizens of non-European countries have been on the rise since 2012, increasing from 431,000 applications in 2013 to 627,000 in 2014 and around 1.3 million in both 2015 and 2016. However, the number of first-time asylum applicants fell slightly in 2016. A first-time asylum applicant is a person who is applying for asylum for the first time in an EU member state. This number excludes repeat applications in that member state, and thus correctly reflects the number of newly arrived persons applying for asylum in that state (Eurostat).

Syrians accounted for the largest number of applicants in 13 of the 28 EU member states. Syrians started to seek asylum outside their region in 2012. These attempts are attributed to the ongoing conflict, the difficult living conditions in neighboring countries, and the few resettlement slots offered by developing countries. Germany and Sweden received the greatest number of asylum applications from Syrian nationals. From 2012 to 2014, Germany received 61,885 Syrian asylum claims and Sweden received 55,210. In 2014 alone, Germany received 41,100 applications, more than three times as many as in 2013 (12,855), and five times as many as in 2012 (7,930). In Sweden, 30,750 Syrian asylum claims were made in 2014, compared to 16,540 claims in 2013 and 7,920 in 2012 (Ostrand 2015:269–271).

Germany not only received the highest number of asylum applications but also provided the highest first-instance decision rate. The Eurostat figures include data on first-instance decisions but not on final decisions taken in appeal or review. In 2016, there were 1.1 million first-instance decisions in all EU member states, compared to 593,000 in 2015. The largest number of decisions was taken in Germany, amounting to 57% of the total first-instance decisions in the EU-28 in 2016 (Eurostat).

Table 1 shows the number of asylum applications received by nine of the EU-28 countries in 2016 as well as the rate of acceptance. According to the table, Germany is the only EU country that received over 500,000 applications. Eight other European countries (France, Greece, Hungary, Italy, Austria, Sweden, Netherlands, and the United Kingdom) received between 30,000 and 75,000. The rest of the EU countries (not included in this table) received between 2,000 and 15,000. Moreover, 70% of first-instance decisions in Germany were positive and 40% of the decisions resulted in refugee status.

**Resettlement.** In 2013, the UNHCR urged EU countries to increase the number of places for resettlement. It requested the resettlement of some 10,000 Syrians in 2013 and another 30,000 in 2014. Many non-traditional resettlement countries, including Germany, Austria, France, Spain, Luxemburg, Hungary, and Ireland, responded to the UNHCR's call and agreed to resettle Syrian refugees (Bokshi 2013:5). According to the UNHCR's statistics, 2,576 Syrians were referred by the UNHCR to third countries for resettlement during the period January 2012 to September 2014. Of this number, 60% (1,545) were resettled in four

## Table 1: Applications by Syrians and non-Syrians to nine EU countries in 2016

| Countries | Number of applications submitted by Syrians | Number of applications submitted by other nationalities | % granted refugee status | % granted other forms of protection | % rejected |
|---|---|---|---|---|---|
| Austria | 8,730 | 31,130 | 58% | 14% | 28% |
| France | 4,670 | 71,320 | 22% | 13% | 65% |
| Germany | 266,250 | 456,015 | 40% | 28% | 32% |
| Greece | 26,630 | 23,245 | 23% | 4% | 73% |
| Hungary | 4,875 | 23,340 | 3% | 4% | 93% |
| Italy | 0 | 57,335 | 5% | 60% | 35% |
| Netherlands | 2,865 | 16,420 | 35% | 37% | 28% |
| Sweden | 4,610 | 17,620 | 28% | 42% | 30% |
| United Kingdom | 0 | 38,290 | 28% | 39% | 33% |

Source: Eurostat

countries: Germany, Sweden, the United Kingdom, and the US. However, Germany absorbed more than half of this number (941), while the United Kingdom only accepted 2% (34) (Ostrand 2015:269–271).

## Germany's Asylum Policy

The right to asylum is codified in Article 16 of the Basic Law. According to this article, anyone persecuted on political grounds shall enjoy the right of asylum in Germany, a right that was meant to protect those fleeing political persecution under communist regimes. This absolute right to political asylum enabled Germany to offer protection to a considerable number of refugees, particularly those from the former Yugoslavia. Facing growing immigration pressures, Article 16 was amended in 1993. The amendment excluded applications for asylum from countries that Germany considered 'safe countries,' which included EU member states as well as Austria, the Czech Republic, Finland, Norway, Poland, Sweden, and Switzerland, which were not part of the EU then.

Moreover, the amendment ended the automatic granting of refugee status to applicants from 'unsafe countries' and requested proof of persecution for granting refugee status (Hailbronner 1994:159–164).

In addition to the constitution, the right to asylum is codified in national legislation through the incorporation of the 1951 convention and the relevant EU laws and regulations. The two most important immigration laws are the Asylum Act and the Residence Act. The Asylum Act regulates the process of granting and denying asylum. According to the act, asylum seekers who are permitted to enter Germany or who are found in the country without a residence permit are allowed to submit an asylum application to the responsible branch of the Federal Office for Migration and Refugees (BAMF). An asylum seeker can be denied entry if he/she is coming from a country recognized by Germany as safe, if Germany is not the country that is supposed to register his/her application (Dublin Regulation), or if he/she constitutes a threat to the general public. The Residence Act, on the other hand, regulates the entry, stay, exit, and employment of foreigners. Since Germany had never had a resettlement program, the admission of resettled refugees is regulated by Article 23 (2) of the Residence Act, which enables the federal government, in consultation with the government of the concerned German state, to admit foreigners into the country by issuing either a temporary residence permit or a permanent settlement permit, depending on the approval for admission ("Refugee Law and Policy: Germany").

**Amendments to the Asylum and Residency Acts in response to the Syrian crisis.** Despite Germany's open-door policy that enabled it to process a considerable number of applications by Syrian asylum seekers, amendments were introduced to both the Asylum and the Residency Acts between 2015 and 2017. Many German refugee rights organizations regard these amendments as overly restrictive.

The amendments were a response to new EU regulations and directives introduced in 2013 to the Common European Asylum System. A regulation is a binding act that must be applied in the same manner by all member states, while a directive is a broader goal for which each member state can set its own laws to achieve. Regulation 603/2013 added a component to the European Dactyloscopy (Eurodac), the

European Union Fingerprint Database, for law enforcement, giving authorities the right to compare fingerprints linked to criminal investigations with those contained in Eurodac. Regulation 1052/2013 is concerned with the border surveillance system known as Eurosur to improve control at external EU borders. Regulation 604/2013, known as Dublin Regulation III, allows asylum seekers to appeal a Dublin decision.[2] Directive 2013/33 deals with reception conditions. The asylum procedure Directive 2013/32 provides common procedures for granting and withdrawing international protection, improving the minimum standards that were established by Directive 85 in 2005 and introduced the 'accelerated procedures' and 'safe country' options (EUR-Lex). The German Asylum Act was amended on October 24, 2015 with an article known as "Asylum Procedure Acceleration Act" or Asylum Package I. The article includes four important provisions that affect asylum seekers. The first is that it accelerates the asylum process for certain applicants, which is regarded as the primary aim of the act. Accelerating the asylum process could have a negative impact because it reduces the time for assessing the asylum application. Second, it increases the budget allocated to the states on the grounds that they bear the cost of hosting refugees and calls upon each state to improve the integration process. Third, the act increases the list of countries classified as safe, to include Albania, Kosovo, and Montenegro. Finally, the act substitutes in-kind benefits for cash benefits for asylum seekers whose applications have been denied or who have failed to submit valid documentation. The reason is that these asylum seekers need basic subsistence until they either are deported or submit valid documents (Asylum Procedure Acceleration Act).

Asylum Package II was debated in the parliament throughout 2016 and was finally passed in March 2017. Like the earlier act, it aimed to accelerate the asylum application process for certain types of asylum applicants, for example, applicants from safe countries of origin, follow-up applicants, or applicants without documents. According to the new act, these claims for asylum should be evaluated within a week. One more week is given to the applicant to appeal the decision, and the administrative court is given an additional week to decide on the appeal. All in all, the whole process would not take more than three

---

2   European Commission. "Country Responsible or Asylum Application [Dublin]."

weeks (Asylum Procedure Acceleration Act). The act has been criticized because it would have a negative impact on people without identification papers (such as Palestinians from Syria or Afghanis from Iran), those who have lost their documents during the journey, or those who are in need of protection but excluded at first because they are coming from countries classified as 'safe.' The act also suspended family reunification for refugees with subsidiary protection status for a period of two years; decreased monthly cash benefits; and defined the provisions on suspending deportations for health reasons, indicating that suspension is only allowed if there is proof that the foreigner is suffering from a life-threatening illness that could worsen in case of deportation (German National Contact Point for the European Migration Network 2016:37).

A number of other acts concerning asylum were also passed in 2016. For example, the act on faster expulsion of criminal foreigners gave the authorities the right to refuse applicants on the basis of suspected criminality, and the integration act indicated the reasons for the inadmissibility of an asylum application. In addition to inadmissibility because of the Dublin Regulation, the act included other grounds that were criticized as restricting the right to asylum (German National Contact Point for the European Migration Network 2016). Amendments were also introduced to Section 11 of the Residence Act which regulate the ban on entry and residence. On August 1, 2015, the Act Redefining the Right to Remain and Termination of Residence was introduced, giving the federal office the responsibility for setting a time limit for asylum seekers whose ban on entry has become effective. The act also ordered a ban on entry and residency for applicants from countries designated as 'safe' (Bans on Entry and Residence). At the same time, it granted residence permits to persons who can prove that they are well integrated after a period of eight years, and to well-integrated minors after four years. Thus, on one hand, the law facilitated residency for those already living in Germany, but on the other hand, it restricted entry for newly arrived asylum seekers ("Bundestag Passed the New Asylum Law").

## The Role of Interest Groups

As we have seen, Germany's initial response, as compared to other European countries, was welcoming and accepting. This is apparent from the number of asylum applications received and the rate of refugee status recognition. On the other hand, the amendments introduced to both the Asylum and Residency Acts are restrictive. However, Germany was obliged to adopt these amendments, since EU directives were to be incorporated into member states' legislation by July 2015. The European Commission sent a letter of formal notice to Germany on September 23, 2015 for failing to do so. The adoption of Asylum Package I in October 2015 was a response to the September letter (European Commission 2015).

The process of incorporating the directives into Germany's national legislation was characterized by strong debate. For example, the individual states, which are bearing the responsibilities of financing reception centers, were against a more liberal reception law, while refugee interest groups were in favor of more liberal laws (Dorrenbacher and Mastenbroek 2017:1). Refugee and human rights interest groups were against strict asylum regulations, while the right-wing movement was advocating stricter policies. The next section will explain the activities and tactics used by each of the interest groups, the impact of such activities, and the role they played during the discussion of the amendments.

**i) Refugee rights organizations.** As mentioned earlier, refugee rights organizations have defined organizational structures and large numbers of members. Their ability to recruit members not only provides them with financial independence but also gives them organizational legitimacy. Refugee rights organizations, like other interest groups, can be invited to participate in the committees debating the proposed bills to the parliament, thus contributing directly to policies, and some of them are registered at the Bundestag ("Anlage 2 der Geschäftsordnung").

**Tactics used to promote refugee rights.** Refugee rights organizations have always been actively engaged in campaigning to encourge the admission of refugees to Germany and to protect their rights. One of the most successful campaigns organized by Pro Asyl, the largest refugee organization in Germany, is the "Save Me" campaign, which was launched in 2008 with the objective of enabling asylum seekers to reach Germany safely. Within three years, local "Save Me" campaigns successfully made over 50 cities and districts sign council agreements on the active admission of refugees into their communities ("Save Me

Kampagne"). When advocating for refugee issues by means of campaigns and protests, refugee rights organizations use a number of tactics to encourage people to identify with the refugees. They highlight commonalities, downplay differerences, and rely on awakening the human feelings of individuals. They rely strongly on the label "Human." The slogans used in their campaign include, for example, "No human is illegal" and "Unity in diversity" (Rommel 2017:143–145).

In addition to campaigns, refugee rights organizations intervene in public debates, produce publications and briefings on topics relevant to refugee policy and human rights at the German and European levels, and lobby for asylum policies defending refugees' rights and interests. Members of refugee rights organizations take part in debates in the parliament, as well as issuing statements and legal opinions (Pro Asyl website).

**Role during the discussion of the amendment.** EU directives, unlike regulations, are binding only with respect to the results to be achieved; member states are allowed to take local contexts into consideration when translating the directives into national law (Dorrenbacher and Mastenbroek 2017:9). Accordingly, refugee and human rights organizations advocated against strict adherence to the directives by directing attention to their possible negative impact. In February 2012, Pro Asyl issued a statement against incorporating the Reception Conditions Directive with its detention regime that would tighten up asylum law (Statement by Pro Asyl on the Planned EU Asylum Package 2016:4). In addition to refugee and human rights organizations, business associations in Germany have also played a role with regard to hosting refugees. Businesses in Germany, particularly smaller ones, suffer from a lack of skilled workers. The influx of refugees was thus perceived by businesses not as a problem but as an opportunity to obtain skilled workers. Therefore, business associations, particularly those representing the interests of small and medium-sized businesses, advocated for welcoming, accepting, and integrating refugees into the labor market. However, they did not expect the number of refugees to be as big as it was. In addition, it became evident after a while that the process of integrating refugees into the labor market was much more complicated than originally anticipated. As a result, the business organizations eventually advocated for policies that would enable integration of refugees already in Germany while calling for stricter entry policies (Dannenbring 2018).

Business associations were in close contact with the government, negotiating the terms and conditions of the new integration law to facilitate the integration of refugees into the labor market. The Central Association of German Crafts (Zentralverband des Deutschen Handwerks [ZDH]), for example, played a major role in integrating the 3+2 rule, concerning the legal status of apprentices in Germany, into the integration law. The idea is that if an asylum seeker is granted an apprenticeship in a German business, he cannot be deported for five years, three of which were to be spent in the apprenticeship and an additional two in the company that provided the apprenticeship (Dannenbring 2018).

At the same time, the four largest German associations published a joint statement supporting the restrictive asylum amendments represented in the Asylum Package II on the basis that the German economy would not be able to integrate additional refugees. The four associations that drafted the joint statement were the Central Association of German Crafts, the German Industry Association, the German Employers Association, and the German Employment Authority (Dannenbring 2018).

**ii) Xenophobic anti-migrant groups.** Although there are some registered organizations, like PEGIDA, that advocate for nationalist ideology and strict asylum policies, most anti-migrant groups lack organizational structure because of the legal restrictions imposed on racist organizations. Moreover, those that do have an organizational structure, like PEDIGA, have few members, and most of their supporters engage in their activities without formal membership. Despite that, their influence on policies should not be underestimated, as many of their members are well connected with right-wing conservative politicians and parties as well as with similar groups in other parts of Europe.

**Tactics used to militate against refugees and minorities.** The main strategies used by PEGIDA and other extreme right groups are protest and demonstration. In their protests, they portray the 'other' as a threat, emphasizing their differences and strangeness. The most important activity of PEGIDA is the regular Monday demonstration (Montagsdemonstrationen) in Dresden, the capital of Saxony. In 2015, it was estimated that the demonstration included between 10,000 and 15,000 participants. To promote their cause, they use propaganda measures that include providing misleading or exaggerated information to the public and demonizing anyone who tries to refute it. Any media or press outlet that asserts the opposite is painted as illegitimate "Lügenpresse" ('lying media'), and politicians working against the demands of PEGIDA are accused of treason (Jennerjahn 2016).

The strategies used by PEGIDA, unfortunately, are not without consequences. Encroachments on migrants and their shelters have more than tripled since the initiation of PEGIDA demonstrations. Protests and demonstrations against building shelters for refugees have also increased. For example, Berlin witnessed demonstrations opposing the construction of three refugee shelters in its surrounding suburban districts of Pankow, Marzahn-Hellersdorf, and Treptow-Köpenick (Pro Asyl 2014/2015:8).

The impact of PEGIDA's activities on public perception was documented by a study done by the economic center in Berlin. The study surveyed participants at PEGIDA demonstrations. The final report states that 48.7% of the participants place themselves in the center-right orientation of the political spectrum, 33.3% consider themselves right wing, and 1.7% place themselves in the extreme right wing. When asked about which party they had voted for in the past, 33% indicated that they had voted for the Alternative for Germany (AfD), a new right-wing party that was founded in February 2013; meanwhile, 21% had voted for the CDU. When asked whom they intended to vote for in the upcoming elections, an overwhelming 89% stated that they would vote for the AfD; 5% indicated that they intend to vote for the NPD, which is even farther to the right; all other parties together accounted for a mere 5%. The study argued that this shift is an indication of the increased impact of PEGIDA's ideas, as well as a demonstration of how withdrawing one's vote can be used as a political mechanism to impact policies. Those who previously voted for the CDU might be trying to withdraw their vote as a strategy to compel their party to change their stated policy (Jennerjahn 2016).

**Role during the discussion of the amendment.** For a bill to be adopted by the parliament, it usually goes through three readings. The first reading does not always include a debate. Its purpose is to designate one or more committees to deliberate the bill and prepare for the debate in the second reading. Committees are made up of members from all parliamentary groups, who are given the task of studying the bill and making recommendations. Members of the committee (or committees) can invite representatives of interest groups and experts to the committee meetings to discuss the proposed bill ("Passage of Legislation").

As mentioned above, Asylum Package I was passed in October 2015 and Asylum Package II in March 2017. During that time, the ruling party was the CDU, in coalition with the SPD, and the opposition parties were the Greens and the Left Party. The right wing was not represented because of their inability to meet the 5% threshold. Therefore, the parliamentary groups that made up the committees and invited interest groups did not include right-wing parties. Accordingly, it can be argued that the right wing in Germany did not have a direct impact on the passing of the amendment.

**iii) Home Town Associations.** Home Town Associations, in Germany and elsewhere in Europe, are usually concerned strictly with their own communities: either with issues related to their countries of origin or with facilitating integration of their communities in the host countries. Only rarely have the Home Town Associations of different migrant communities come together to address the general conditions of all migrants.

In the last few years, however, some attempts to coordinate between different groups of migrants in Europe have started to appear. For example, in 2012, a movement known as the "Refugee Movement: News from Inside" was initiated after the suicide of the Iranian refugee Muhammed Rahsapar at the refugee camp in Würzburg. Following the incident, refugees from other camps in Germany came together and marched in a protest movement to Berlin. In Berlin, they set up a protest camp at Oranienplatz in Kreuzberg. The aim of the camp was to increase awareness of the refugees' problems in German society, and to resist what they described as "discriminatory laws." In 2014, they engaged in a protest march from Strasbourg to Brussels, seeking to bring their demands to the European level. Since then, they have been actively engaged in protests and demonstrations. They also have their own website where they share news and events. According to the website, they have managed to bring the 'refugee problem' to the political agenda. However, although they claim that they cover all groups of migrants, they mostly include African refugees (Refugee Movement, News from Inside).

Apart from these specific activities, nothing else is documented about activism on the part of migrants and refugees to promote their cause in Germany. Consequently, there is no indication that they have an impact on the policies targeting them.

## Conclusion

Germany adopted an open-door policy toward the Syrian refugee crisis. This is apparent not only from the high number of asylum applications, but also from the high rate of refugee status recognition. Although the amendments introduced in 2015 and 2017 restricted access to asylum, Germany was obliged to adopt them, as they were imposed by the EU as part of administering the Common European Asylum system. As explained, the EU directives and regulations of 2013 were not incorporated into German legislation until October 2015. This chapter has attempted to understand the reason behind the more generous open-door policy adopted by Germany as compared to other European countries. It used the theory of the Social Construction of the Targeted Population, which argues that the degree of either positive or negative impact on the social group targeted by a policy will depend on the political power of that group. To evaluate the political power of refugees, it was assumed that their power could be measured by the number of interest groups working on their behalf as compared to those working against them.

In terms of resources, pro-migrant groups have clear organizational structures and large numbers of members. Having official registered members not only provides them with a steady source of financial resources, but also gives them organizational legitimacy. Xenophobic anti-migrant groups in Germany, by contrast, lack such legitimacy. The German legal system prohibits the establishment of organizations that

# Conclusion

engage in activities promoting racism. As a result, right-wing extremism expresses itself mostly through movements rather than groups with a well-defined structure. These movements gained momentum in protesting Germany's open-door policy toward refugees, as indicated in the increased number of so-called 'civil initiatives' against the building of refugee camps.

In terms of lobbying strategies, although the anti-refugee movement has no organizational structure, it is well connected with the right-wing party, and is thus able to engage in internal lobbying, exactly like the pro-refugee groups. However, since the recent restrictive amendments were passed in 2015 and early 2017, before the AfD party gained seats in the parliament, it is reasonable to assume that the right-wing anti-migrant movement had no direct impact on the adoption of the amendments. Their effect is instead mostly indirect, by influencing public opinion and thus creating a preference for restrictive policies. This translates into voter support in parliamentary elections.

The interview conducted with the Central Association of German Crafts for this study highlighted the role played by German business associations in both the initial welcoming response and the strict asylum packages adopted in 2015 and 2017. Initially, the influx of refugees was perceived by businesses in Germany as an opportunity to obtain skilled workers. Therefore the business associations, particularly those representing the interests of small and medium-sized businesses, advocated for accepting refugees and integrating them into the labor market. However, with the increase in the number of refugees and the inability of the labor market to absorb them, they started to advocate for policies that would support the integration of those already in Germany but enforce stricter entry policies.

Based on this study, it is reasonable to conclude that refugee-rights interest groups, as well as business associations in Germany, were behind the initial welcoming response and open-door policy. The increase in the number of refugees, the difficulty of integrating them into the labor market, the rise of anti-migrant movements like PEGIDA, and the pressure imposed by the EU were reasons behind the restrictive policies that followed. Further research is needed for more in-depth analysis of the role of business associations and ways to facilitate the integration of refugees into the labor markets of host countries.

## References

"Anlage 2 der Geschäftsordnung des Deutschen Bundestages—Registrierung von Verbänden und deren Vertretern." Deutscher Bundestag. https://www.bundestag.de/parlament/aufgaben/rechtsgrundlagen/go_btg/anlage2/245180

Asylum Procedure Acceleration Act. 2015. *German Federal Gazette*, October 20 (BGBl I 1722).

Bans on Entry and Residence. Federal Office for Migration and Refugees. https://www.bamf.de/EN/Fluechtlingsschutz/AblaufAsylv/AusgangVerfahren/EinreiseAufenthaltsverbote/einreise-aufenthaltsverbote.html

Baroni, L., C. Brendan, A. Chalmers, M. Luz, and A. Rasmussen. 2014. "Defining and Classifying Interest Groups," *Interest Groups & Advocacy*, 3: 141–159.

Bokshi, Elona. 2013. "Refugee Resettlement in the EU: The Capacity to Do It Better and to Do It More." Robert Schuman Center for Advanced Studies, European University Institute, KNOW RESET Research Report 4.

"Bundestag Passed the New Asylum Law: What Will Change." Refugee Movement: News from Inside. http://oplatz.net/in-english-latest-changes-in-the-asylum-law/

Caritas Germany. http://www.caritas-germany.org/focus/currentissues/what-does-caritas-do-for-refugees-in-germany

Dannenbring, Jan. 2018. Skype interview with Zentralverband des Deutschen Handwerks, March 1.

Dorrenbacher, N., and E. Mastenbroek. 2017. "Passing the Buck: Analyzing the Delegation of Discretion after Transposition of European Union Law," *Regulation and Governance*, 2017: 1–16. doi:10.1111/rego.12153

EUR-Lex: Access to European Union Law. https://eur-lex.europa.eu/homepage.html

European Commission. 2015. "Responsibility in Managing the Refugee Crisis: European Commission Adopts 40 Infringement Decisions to Make European Asylum System Work," September 23. http://europa.eu/rapid/press-release_IP-15-5699_en.htm

European Commission. "Country Responsible or Asylum Application (Dublin)." https://ec.europa.eu/home-affairs/what-we-do/policies/asylum/examination-of-applicants_en

European Council on Refugees and Exiles (ECRE). http://www.ecre.org/
European Resettlement Network. "Germany." http://www.resettlement.eu/country/germany
Eurostat."MigrationandMigrantPopulationStatistics."http://ec.europa.eu/eurostat/statistics-explained/index.php/Migration_and_migrant_population_statistics
Flentje, J. 2015. "Wie nehmen Interessengruppen Einfluss auf den deutschen Bundestagswahlkampf?" Unpublished PhD dissertation: Faculty of Social Sciences, University of Mannheim.
Geoffrey, R. 2009. *German Politics Today*. Manchester: Manchester University Press.
German Criminal Code. https://germanlawarchive.iuscomp.org/?p=752#BI
German National Contact Point for the European Migration Network (EMN). 2017. "Migration, Integration, Asyl." Bundesamt für Migration und Flüchtlinge, 1–108. http://www.bamf.de/SharedDocs/Anlagen/EN/Publikationen/EMN/Politikberichte/emn-politikbericht-2016-germany.pdf?__blob=publicationFile
Hailbronner, K. 1994. "Asylum Law Reform in the German Constitution," *American University International Law Review*, 9: 159–179.
Hoehl, S. 1995. "Neo-Nazism and the Right-Wing Movement in Germany: Should Offenders Be Punished Severely?" *Current Issues in Criminal Justice*, 7: 94–98. http://www.austlii.edu.au/au/journals/CICrimJust/1995/25.pdf
Hoeks, Gay. 2016. "PEGIDA under Closer Scrutiny: How a Regional Protest Movement Evolved into a Pan-European Phenomenon." Unpublished MA thesis, Leiden University, European Union Studies.
Ingram, H., A. Schneider, and P. DeLeon. 2007. "Social Construction and Policy Design." In P. Sabatier, ed. *Theories of the Policy Process*, 93–128. Boulder, CO: Westview Press.
Jennerjahn, M. 2016. "Sachsen als Entstehungsort der völkerrassistischen Bewegung PEGIDA." In S. Braun, A. Geisler, and M. Gerster, ed. *Strategien der extremen Rechten*, 533–558. Wiesbaden: Springer.
Knight, B. 2017. "German Issues in a Nutshell: PEGIDA." Deutsche Welle. http://www.dw.com/en/german-issues-in-a-nutshell-pegida/a-39124630
Macedo de Jesus, A. 2010. "Policy-Making Process and Interest Groups: How Do Local Government Associations Influence Policy Outcome

in Brazil and the Netherlands?" *Brazilian Political Science Review* 4: 69–101. https://repub.eur.nl/pub/76055/Metis_201241.pdf

Martin, N. 2012. "Clamping Down on Right-Wing Associations." Deutsche Welle. http://www.dw.com/en/clamping-down-on-right-wing-associations/a-16193449

Mayer, M. 2016. "Germany Response to the Refugee Situation: Remarkable Leadership or Fait Accompli?" Bertelsmann Foundation. http://www.bfna.org/research/germanys-response-to-the-refugee-situation-remarkable-leadership-or-fait-accompli/

Orozco, M., and E. Garcia-Zanello. 2009. "Hometown Associations: Transnationalism, Philanthropy, and Development," *Brown Journal of World Affairs*, 15: 57–73.

Ostrand, N. 2015. "The Syrian Refugee Crisis: A Comparison of Responses by Germany, Sweden, the United Kingdom, and the United States," *Journal on Migration and Human Security*, 3: 255–279. doi: https://doi.org/10.14240/jmhs.v3i3.51

Der Paritätische Wohlfahrtsverband. http://www.der-paritaetische.de/verband/ueber-uns/

"Passage of Legislation." Deutscher Bundestag. https://www.bundestag.de/en/parliament/function/legislation/passage/245704

Pro Asyl website. www.proasyl.de

Prol Asyl. 2014. Brochure explaining right-wing mobilization and how to react to it. https://www.amadeu-antonio-stiftung.de/w/files/pdfs/broschuere_brandstifter_internet.pdf

———. 2014/2015. "Annual Report." https://www.proasyl.de/wp-content/uploads/2015/12/PRO_ASYL_Taetigkeitsbericht_2014-2015.pdf

"Refugee Law and Policy: Germany." Library of Congress. https://www.loc.gov/law/help/refugee-law/germany.php

Refugee Movement: News from Inside. https://oplatz.net

Rommel, I. 2017. "We Are the People: Refugee 'Crisis' and the Drag-Effects of Social Habitus in German Society," *Historical Social Research*, 42: 133–154.

"Save Me Kampagne." Pro Asyl. https://www.proasyl.de/thema/aufnahmeprogramme/save-me-kampagne/

Siegel, M., N. Ragab, and L. Rahmeier. 2017. "Mapping the Syrian Diaspora in Germany: Contributions to Peace, Reconstruction, and

Potentials for Collaboration with German Development Cooperation." Maastricht School of Governance. https://www.merit.unu.edu/publications/uploads/1487758705.pdf

Statement by Pro Asyl on the Planned EU Asylum Package. 2016. November. https://www.proasyl.de/wp-content/uploads/2015/12/Kommentar_Asylpaket-EU-PRO-ASYL.pdf

## About the Contributors

**Dr. Ibrahim Awad** is professor of practice and director of the Center for Migration and Refugee Studies, the American University in Cairo.

**Maysa Ayoub** is manager and adjunct faculty in the Center for Migration and Refugee Studies, the American University in Cairo.

**Dr. Angelos Dalachanis** is research fellow at the French School of Athens.

**Dr. Gerda Heck** is assistant professor of sociology, the American University in Cairo.

**Dr. Alexandra Parrs** is research associate at CeMIS, University of Antwerp and American University in Brussels.

**Dr. Gerasimos Tsourapas** is lecturer in Middle East Politics, Department of Political Science and International Studies, University of Birmingham.

**Dr. Joseph John Viscomi** is lecturer in modern European history in the Department of History, Classics and Archaeology at Birkbeck, University of London.

# CAIRO PAPERS IN SOCIAL SCIENCE

**Volume One**
1 *Women, Health and Development*, Cynthia Nelson, ed.
2 *Democracy in Egypt*, Ali E. Hillal Dessouki, ed.
3 *Mass Communications and the October War*, Olfat Hassan Agha
4 *Rural Resettlement in Egypt*, Helmy Tadros
5 *Saudi Arabian Bedouin*, Saad E. Ibrahim and Donald P. Cole

**Volume Two**
1 *Coping with Poverty in a Cairo Community*, Andrea B. Rugh
2 *Modernization of Labor in the Arab Gulf*, Enid Hill
3 *Studies in Egyptian Political Economy*, Herbert M. Thompson
4 *Law and Social Change in Contemporary Egypt*, Cynthia Nelson and Klaus Friedrich Koch, eds.
5 *The Brain Drain in Egypt*, Saneya Saleh

**Volume Three**
1 *Party and Peasant in Syria*, Raymond Hinnebusch
2 *Child Development in Egypt*, Nicholas V. Ciaccio
3 *Living without Water*, Asaad Nadim et al.
4 *Export of Egyptian School Teachers*, Suzanne A. Messiha
5 *Population and Urbanization in Morocco*, Saad E. Ibrahim

**Volume Four**
1 *Cairo's Nubian Families*, Peter Geiser
2, 3 *Symposium on Social Research for Development: Proceedings, Social Research Center*
4 *Women and Work in the Arab World*, Earl L. Sullivan and Karima Korayem

**Volume Five**
1 *Ghagar of Sett Guiranha: A Study of a Gypsy Community in Egypt*, Nabil Sobhi Hanna
2 *Distribution of Disposal Income and the Impact of Eliminating Food Subsidies in Egypt*, Karima Korayem
3 *Income Distribution and Basic Needs in Urban Egypt*, Amr Mohie el-Din

**Volume Six**
1   *The Political Economy of Revolutionary Iran,* Mihssen Kadhim
2   *Urban Research Strategies in Egypt,* Richard A. Lobban, ed.
3   *Non-alignment in a Changing World,* Mohammed el-Sayed Selim, ed.
4   *The Nationalization of Arabic and Islamic Education in Egypt: Dar al-Alum and al-Azhar,* Lois A. Arioan

**Volume Seven**
1   *Social Security and the Family in Egypt,* Helmi Tadros
2   *Basic Needs, Inflation and the Poor of Egypt,* Myrette el-Sokkary
3   *The Impact of Development Assistance on Egypt,* Earl L. Sullivan, ed.
4   *Irrigation and Society in Rural Egypt,* Sohair Mehanna, Richard Huntington, and Rachad Antonius

**Volume Eight**
1, 2   *Analytic Index of Survey Research in Egypt,* Madiha el-Safty, Monte Palmer, and Mark Kennedy

**Volume Nine**
1   *Philosophy, Ethics and Virtuous Rule,* Charles E. Butterworth
2   *The 'Jihad': An Islamic Alternative in Egypt,* Nemat Guenena
3   *The Institutionalization of Palestinian Identity in Egypt,* Maha A. Dajani
4   *Social Identity and Class in a Cairo Neighborhood,* Nadia A. Taher

**Volume Ten**
1   *Al-Sanhuri and Islamic Law,* Enid Hill
2   *Gone for Good,* Ralph Sell
3   *The Changing Image of Women in Rural Egypt,* Mona Abaza
4   *Informal Communities in Cairo: The Basis of a Typology,* Linda Oldham, Haguer el Hadidi, and Hussein Tamaa

**Volume Eleven**
1   *Participation and Community in Egyptian New Lands: The Case of South Tahrir,* Nicholas Hopkins et al.
2   *Palestinian Universities under Occupation,* Antony T. Sullivan
3   *Legislating Infitah: Investment, Foreign Trade and Currency Laws,* Khaled M. Fahmy
4   *Social History of an Agrarian Reform Community in Egypt,* Reem Saad

## Volume Twelve
1. *Cairo's Leap Forward: People, Households, and Dwelling Space*, Fredric Shorter
2. *Women, Water, and Sanitation: Household Water Use in Two Egyptian Villages*, Samiha el-Katsha et al.
3. *Palestinian Labor in a Dependent Economy: Women Workers in the West Bank Clothing Industry*, Randa Siniora
4. *The Oil Question in Egyptian–Israeli Relations, 1967–1979: A Study in International Law and Resource Politics*, Karim Wissa

## Volume Thirteen
1. *Squatter Markets in Cairo*, Helmi R. Tadros, Mohamed Feteeha, and Allen Hibbard
2. *The Sub-culture of Hashish Users in Egypt: A Descriptive Analytic Study*, Nashaat Hassan Hussein
3. *Social Background and Bureaucratic Behavior in Egypt*, Earl L. Sullivan, el Sayed Yassin, Ali Leila, and Monte Palmer
4. *Privatization: The Egyptian Debate*, Mostafa Kamel el-Sayyid

## Volume Fourteen
1. *Perspectives on the Gulf Crisis*, Dan Tschirgi and Bassam Tibi
2. *Experience and Expression: Life among Bedouin Women in South Sinai*, Deborah Wickering
3. *Impact of Temporary International Migration on Rural Egypt*, Atef Hanna Nada
4. *Informal Sector in Egypt*, Nicholas S. Hopkins, ed.

## Volume Fifteen
1. *Scenes of Schooling: Inside a Girls' School in Cairo*, Linda Herrera
2. *Urban Refugees: Ethiopians and Eritreans in Cairo*, Dereck Cooper
3. *Investors and Workers in the Western Desert of Egypt: An Exploratory Survey*, Naeim Sherbiny, Donald Cole, and Nadia Makary
4. *Environmental Challenges in Egypt and the World*, Nicholas S. Hopkins, ed.

## Volume Sixteen
1. *The Socialist Labor Party: A Case Study of a Contemporary Egyptian Opposition Party*, Hanaa Fikry Singer
2. *The Empowerment of Women: Water and Sanitation Initiatives in Rural Egypt*, Samiha el Katsha and Susan Watts
3. *The Economics and Politics of Structural Adjustment in Egypt: Third Annual Symposium*

4   *Experiments in Community Development in a Zabbaleen Settlement,* Marie Assaad and Nadra Garas

**Volume Seventeen**
1   *Democratization in Rural Egypt: A Study of the Village Local Popular Council,* Hanan Hamdy Radwan
2   *Farmers and Merchants: Background for Structural Adjustment in Egypt,* Sohair Mehanna, Nicholas S. Hopkins, and Bahgat Abdelmaksoud
3   *Human Rights: Egypt and the Arab World, Fourth Annual Symposium*
4   *Environmental Threats in Egypt: Perceptions and Actions,* Salwa S. Gomaa, ed.

**Volume Eighteen**
1   *Social Policy in the Arab World,* Jacqueline Ismael and Tareq Y. Ismael
2   *Workers, Trade Unions and the State in Egypt: 1984–1989,* Omar el-Shafie
3   *The Development of Social Science in Egypt: Economics, History and Sociology; Fifth Annual Symposium*
4   *Structural Adjustment, Stabilization Policies and the Poor in Egypt,* Karima Korayem

**Volume Nineteen**
1   *Nilopolitics: A Hydrological Regime, 1870–1990,* Mohamed Hatem el-Atawy
2   *Images of the Other: Europe and the Muslim World before 1700,* David R. Blanks et al.
3   *Grass Roots Participation in the Development of Egypt,* Saad Eddin Ibrahim et al.
4   *The Zabbalin Community of Muqattam,* Elena Volpi and Doaa Abdel Motaal

**Volume Twenty**
1   *Class, Family, and Power in an Egyptian Village,* Samer el-Karanshawy
2   *The Middle East and Development in a Changing World,* Donald Heisel, ed.
3   *Arab Regional Women's Studies Workshop,* Cynthia Nelson and Soraya Altorki, eds.
4   *"Just a Gaze": Female Clientele of Diet Clinics in Cairo: An Ethnomedical Study,* Iman Farid Bassyouny

**Volume Twenty-one**
1   *Turkish Foreign Policy during the Gulf War of 1990–1991,* Mostafa Aydin
2   *State and Industrial Capitalism in Egypt,* Samer Soliman
3   *Twenty Years of Development in Egypt (1977–1997): Part I,* Mark C. Kennedy

4   *Twenty Years of Development in Egypt (1977–1997): Part II*, Mark C. Kennedy

**Volume Twenty-two**
1   *Poverty and Poverty Alleviation Strategies in Egypt*, Ragui Assaad and Malak Rouchdy
2   *Between Field and Text: Emerging Voices in Egyptian Social Science*, Seteney Shami and Linda Hererra, eds.
3   *Masters of the Trade: Crafts and Craftspeople in Cairo, 1750–1850*, Pascale Ghazaleh
4   *Discourses in Contemporary Egypt: Politics and Social Issues*, Enid Hill, ed.

**Volume Twenty-three**
1   *Fiscal Policy Measures in Egypt: Public Debt and Food Subsidy*, Gouda Abdel-Khalek and Karima Korayem
2   *New Frontiers in the Social History of the Middle East*, Enid Hill, ed.
3   *Egyptian Encounters*, Jason Thompson, ed.
4   *Women's Perception of Environmental Change in Egypt*, Eman el Ramly

**Volume Twenty-four**
1, 2   *The New Arab Family*, Nicholas S. Hopkins, ed.
3   *An Investigation of the Phenomenon of Polygyny in Rural Egypt*, Laila S. Shahd
4   *The Terms of Empowerment: Islamic Women Activists in Egypt*, Sherine Hafez

**Volume Twenty-five**
1, 2   *Elections in the Middle East: What Do They Mean?* Iman A. Hamdy, ed.
3   *Employment Crisis of Female Graduates in Egypt: An Ethnographic Account*, Ghada F. Barsoum
4   *Palestinian and Israeli Nationalism: Identity Politics and Education in Jerusalem*, Evan S. Weiss

**Volume Twenty-six**
1   *Culture and Natural Environment: Ancient and Modern Middle Eastern Texts*, Sharif S. Elmusa, ed.
2   *Street Children in Egypt: Group Dynamics and Subcultural Constituents*, Nashaat Hussein
3   *IMF–Egyptian Debt Negotiations*, Bessma Momani
4   *Forced Migrants and Host Societies in Egypt and Sudan*, Fabienne Le Houérou

### Volume Twenty-seven
1, 2 *Cultural Dynamics in Contemporary Egypt,* Maha Abdelrahman, Iman A. Hamdy, Malak Rouchdy, and Reem Saad, eds.
3 *The Role of Local Councils in Empowerment and Poverty Reduction,* Solava Ibrahim
4 *Beach Politics: Gender and Sexuality in Dahab,* Mustafa Abdalla

### Volume Twenty-eight
1 *Creating Families across Boundaries: A Case Study of Romanian/Egyptian Mixed Marriages,* Ana Vinea
2, 3 *Pioneering Feminist Anthropology in Egypt: Selected Writings from Cynthia Nelson,* Martina Rieker, ed.
4 *Roses in Salty Soil: Women and Depression in Egypt Today,* Dalia A. Mostafa

### Volume Twenty-nine
1 *Crossing Borders, Shifting Boundaries: Palestinian Dilemmas,* Sari Hanafi, ed.
2, 3 *Political and Social Protest in Egypt,* Nicholas S. Hopkins, ed.
4 *The Experience of Protest: Masculinity and Agency among Sudanese Refugees in Cairo,* Martin T. Rowe

### Volume Thirty
1 *Child Protection Policies in Egypt: A Rights-Based Approach,* Adel Azer, Sohair Mehanna, Mulki Al-Sharmani, and Essam Ali
2 *"The Farthest Place": Social Boundaries in an Egyptian Desert Community,* Joseph Viscomi
3 *The New York Egyptians: Voyages and Dreams,* Yasmine M. Ahmed
4 *The Burden of Resources: Oil and Water in the Gulf and the Nile Basin,* Sharif S. Elmusa, ed.

### Volume Thirty-one
1 *Humanist Perspectives on Sacred Space,* David Blanks, Bradley S. Clough, eds.
2 *Law as a Tool for Empowering Women within Marital Relations: A Case Study of Paternity Lawsuits in Egypt,* Hind Ahmed Zaki
3,4 *Visual Productions of Knowledge: Toward a Different Middle East,* Hanan Sabea, Mark R. Westmoreland, eds.

### Volume Thirty-two
1 *Planning Egypt's New Settlements: The Politics of Spatial Inequities,* Dalia Wahdan

2   *Agrarian Transformation in the Arab World: Persistent and Emerging Challenges,* Habib Ayeb and Reem Saad
3   *Femininity and Dance in Egypt: Embodiment and Meaning in al-Raqs al-Baladi,* Noha Roushdy
4   *Negotiating Space: The Evolution of the Egyptian Street, 2000–2011,* Dimitris Soudias

**Volume Thirty-three**
1   *Masculinities in Egypt and the Arab World: Historical, Literary, and Social Science Perspectives,* Helen Rizzo, ed.
2   *Anthropology in Egypt 1900–1967: Culture, Function, and Reform,* Nicholas S. Hopkins
3   *The Church in the Square: Negotiations of Religion and Revolution at an Evangelical Church in Cairo,* Anna Jeannine Dowell
4   *The Political Economy of the New Egyptian Republic,* Nicholas S. Hopkins, ed.

**Volume Thirty-four**
1   *Egyptian Hip-Hop: Expressions from the Underground,* Ellen R. Weis
2   *Sports and Society in the Middle East,* Nicholas S. Hopkins and Sandrine Gamblin, eds.
3   *Organizing the Unorganized: Migrant Domestic Workers in Lebanon,* Farah Kobaissy
4   *The Food Question in the Middle East,* Malak S. Rouchdy and Iman A. Hamdy, eds.

**Volume Thirty-five**
1   *Oral History in Times of Change: Gender, Documentation, and the Making of Archives,* Hoda Elsadda and Hanan Sabea, eds.

www.ingramcontent.com/pod-product-compliance
Lightning Source LLC
Chambersburg PA
CBHW071919070526
44583CB00016B/2053